Children's Catholic Catechism

BROWN **ROA**
Publishing Media
Dubuque, Iowa

Nihil Obstat
Rev. Richard L. Schaefer

Imprimatur
✠Most Rev. Daniel W. Kucera, O.S.B.
Archbishop of Dubuque
November 2, 1989

The Imprimatur is an official declaration that a book
or pamphlet is free of doctrinal or moral error. No
implication is contained therein that anyone who
granted the Imprimatur agrees with the contents,
opinions, or statements expressed.

Book Team

Publisher—Ernest T. Nedder
Editorial Director—Sandra Hirstein
Editor—Mary Jo Graham
Production Manager—Marilyn Rothenberger
Art Director—Cathy Frantz

Some of the material in this book was taken from
the FOCUS Elementary Program published by
BROWN Publishing–ROA Media.

ISBN 0–697–02872–0

10 9 8 7 6 5 4 3 2 1

Scripture Sources

The New American Bible with Revised New Testament, copyright © 1986
by The Confraternity of Christian Doctrine, Washington, D.C. Published by
Benziger Publishing Company, Mission Hills, CA.

Good News Bible: The Bible in Today's English Version. Old Testament:
© American Bible Society, 1976, New Testament: © American Bible
Society, 1966, 1971, 1976. Maps © United Bible Societies, 1976.

The New Jerusalem Bible. Copyright © 1985 by Darton, Longman & Todd,
Ltd. and Doubleday & Company, Inc.

The Holy Bible: Catholic Students' Edition. Published by J.P. Kennedy &
Sons, New York.

Contents

Section 1

Mystery of God

God is a mystery to people because God can never be totally known by people. We can only know God insofar as God reveals Himself to us. That is why we say that mystery is at the center of Christian faith: the mystery of God the Father who continues to reveal Himself to people; the mystery of Jesus, risen, who shares his life with people in and through the Church; the mystery of the Holy Spirit alive and active among us.

What is at the center of our Catholic faith?

The mystery of the Trinity.

What is the central mystery of the Trinity?

The mystery of the Trinity is that there are three Persons in one God.

Who are the three Persons in one God?

God the Father, God the Son, and God the Holy Spirit.

What do we call the three Persons in one God?

The Blessed Trinity.

What is the most common way we say and show our belief in the three Persons who are God?

The Sign of the Cross.

What is the short prayer of praise we pray to the Trinity?

Glory to the Father, and to the Son, and to the Holy Spirit. As it was in the beginning, is now, and will be forever. Amen.

God the Father

God the Father is the first Person of the Blessed Trinity, the Creator of all that is.

Who is the source of all life?

God is the source of all life.

Why do we call God *Father*?

Because He creates us, provides for us, sustains us, commands us, and guides us; because He is Father toward God the Son.

What do we mean when we say God is Creator?

We mean that God is the maker of all things. God created people.

In whose image did God make people?

God made people in His own image and likeness.

According to Genesis, when did God create people?

On the sixth day of creation, after He had made the world and all else in it.

According to Genesis, what were the names of the first people?

Adam and Eve

Where did Adam and Eve live?

In the Garden of Eden or Paradise.

Did Adam and Eve do all that God asked of them?

No, they disobeyed God and chose to follow their own desires.

What do we call Adam and Eve's sin of disobedience?

Original Sin

Did God the Father disown Adam and Eve after their sin?

No, God made Adam and Eve leave Paradise, but He promised to send a Savior who would restore and bring to fullness what they had lost, namely, union with God.

Why did God make people?

God made people to know Him, to love Him, and to serve Him.

How can people come to know God?

Through creation, the Bible, His Word, Jesus, His people, the Church, and the sacraments.

How can people best come to know God?

We can best come to know God by knowing Jesus.

How do we know that God loves us?

By the many gifts He gives us, and by the fact that He has revealed His love for us.

Does God love us even when we fail?

Yes, God loves us even when we fail.

What great gift does God offer to people?

A share in God's own life.

How do we come to share God's life?

Through the saving power of Jesus.

What is God's life within us called?

Grace

To whom does God offer the gift of His grace?

To all people.

What is the greatest evidence that God wants us to be free?

God's gift of free will; we are free to make our own choices.

What does God want for us?

God wants us to know Him and to be happy in His love.

What is salvation history?

The story of God's saving actions throughout history.

God Created Angels

According to the Bible, what other intelligent beings, in addition to human beings, did God create?

God created angels.

What are angels?

Spirits possessing understanding and free will; God often uses angels as His messengers.

What does the word *angel* mean?

The word *angel* means "one who is sent" or "messenger."

How do we know about angels?

By the many references to them in Scripture and by the teachings of the Church.

Were all angels faithful to God?

Both Scripture and the Church tell us that some angels remained faithful to God and some were unfaithful.

What happened to the angels who were unfaithful to God?

The angels who refused to serve God and fell from grace were banished to hell.

Are any of the faithful angels named in Scripture?

Yes, Michael (Revelation 12:7–9), Gabriel (Luke 1:11–20, 26–38), and Raphael (Tobit 12:6, 15).

How do angels relate to the world?

They are God's ministers sent to protect us. Scripture tells us, "The truth is they are all spirits whose work is service, sent to help those who will be the heirs of salvation." (Hebrews 1:14)

What are Guardian Angels?

Angels who protect people from spiritual and physical dangers and assist them in doing good.

How do we know about Guardian Angels?

Their existence is implied in Scripture and taught by the Church.

How do our Guardian Angels act in our behalf?

By praying for us and by presenting our own petitions to God.

When does the Church celebrate the feast of Guardian Angels?

On October 2

What do we call the fallen angels who were banished to hell?

They are called devils.

What is the name of the leader of the fallen angels?

Satan, or Lucifer, or the Devil.

What does Satan represent?

Satan represents the forces of evil.

What does Satan do?

Satan offers temptations that could lead people to sin.

Why does God allow Satan to tempt people?

To draw us closer to God by giving us the opportunity to show our faith and trust in God.

God the Son

God the Son is the second Person of the Blessed Trinity, God's only-begotten Son, our Savior, Redeemer, and Lord.

Who is the Father's special gift to people?

His Son, Jesus; the Son of God who became a human being.

Who is Jesus?

Jesus is the Son of God, the second Person of the Blessed Trinity, the Word of God made flesh.

Who is the perfect sign of God's love for His people?

Jesus

Was Jesus like other human beings?

Yes, in every way but one—he did not sin.

Why did Jesus never sin?

He chose to use his freedom to never do evil; as a human being, he chose to always be faithful and in union with the divine life which made him who he was.

What does the name *Jesus* mean?

"Yahweh saves"

What are some other names we call Jesus?

We call Jesus *Messiah, Christ, Redeemer.*

What is the *Messiah*?

The Savior whom God promised in the Hebrew Scriptures.

Why do we call Jesus *Messiah*?

Because he is the Savior promised by God.

Why do we call Jesus *Christ*?

Because in Greek *Christ* means "anointed one," which is what Messiah means in the Hebrew language.

Why do we call Jesus *Redeemer*?

Because Jesus brought divine life to humanity and saved humanity from sin.

What are some of the names Jesus called himself?

"Bread of Life" and "The Good Shepherd."

How did Jesus bring divine life to humanity?

By being born in the flesh, dying on the cross, and rising from the dead.

What do we call the Son of God being born in the flesh on earth?

The Incarnation

What do we call Jesus' suffering and death?

The Passion

What do we call Jesus' rising from the dead?

The Resurrection

What do we call Jesus' Passion, Death, and Resurrection?

The Paschal Mystery

What does God show in giving us His Son, Jesus?

In giving us Jesus, God shows His willingness to be one with people.

What does Jesus tell us to call God?

Father

What are the followers of Jesus called?

Christians

Whose life do Christians share through Baptism?

The life of the Trinity.

Who do Christians believe is the most important human being in history?

Jesus, Savior and Lord.

What does believing in Jesus mean?

It means accepting Jesus and his message.

Was Jesus' message contained only in what he said?

No, Jesus' message was also contained in what he did and in how he lived.

Why did Jesus say that he came in history?

Jesus said, "I have come that you might have life—life in all its fullness." (John 10:10)

What is Jesus' public life?

The three years or less during which Jesus taught and preached among the people.

What did Jesus do during his life on earth to show people that he cared about them?

Jesus acted out of love.

What is a miracle?

An extraordinary event showing God's acting in human affairs.

Why did Jesus work miracles?

As a sign that he was God's anointed one sent to free people from evil.

What is Jesus' Law of Love?

"Love one another, just as I love you." (John 15:12)

Who does Jesus call to be his friends?

All people

What does Jesus tell those who want to follow him?

"If anyone wants to come with me, he must forget himself, carry his cross, and follow me." (Mark 8:34)

In what do those who follow Jesus share?

All baptized members of Christ share in his priesthood by the power of the Holy Spirit.

Why is Jesus called *mediator*?

Jesus brings together God and people because he is God and man, human and divine.

What do Christians call Jesus' return to his Father in heaven?

The Ascension

Did Jesus leave his followers alone after the Ascension?

No, he promised to always be with them in the power of the Holy Spirit.

After Jesus rose from the dead and returned to his Father, what gift did he send his followers?

The gift of the Holy Spirit.

The Holy Spirit

The Holy Spirit is the third Person of the Blessed Trinity, who proceeds from the Father and the Son. By the power of the Holy Spirit, God continues His saving works.

Who is the Holy Spirit?

> The spirit of love between the Father and the Son, the third Person of the Blessed Trinity.

Why do we call the Holy Spirit *Reconciler*?

> Because he is the bond that brings Christians together in unity.

Why did Jesus send the Holy Spirit?

> To enable his followers to carry on his work throughout all time and in all places.

When was the fullness of the Holy Spirit given to the Church?

> At Pentecost

Why do we call the Holy Spirit *Sanctifier*?

> Because the Holy Spirit acts in the Church to make people holy.

What are the gifts of the Holy Spirit?

> Wisdom, understanding, counsel (right judgment), fortitude (courage), knowledge, piety (love), and fear of the Lord (awe in the Lord's presence).

What is the gift of wisdom?

> Wisdom enables Christians to recognize good and to know and appreciate what is of value to those who live the Christian life.

What is the gift of understanding?

This gift helps Christians become aware of how and where the Holy Spirit works within us and the Church. It also helps us to be sensitive to one another.

What is the gift of right judgment?

Right judgment helps Christians make good decisions in their own lives and enables them to help others make good decisions in their lives.

What is the gift of fortitude?

This gift (courage) gives Christians strength of character so that they can act rightly and live by Christian principles.

What is the gift of knowledge?

Knowledge enables Christians to use wisely the intelligence that God has given them and to use their gifts and talents to the fullest.

What is the gift of piety?

This gift makes Christians act lovingly toward God and all persons, places, and things related to God.

What is the gift of fear of the Lord?

Fear of the Lord helps Christians acknowledge God's greatness and to avoid that which would offend God.

What are the fruits of the Holy Spirit?

Love, joy, peace, patience, kindness, goodness, faithfulness, humility, and self-control. (Galatians 5:22–23)

Section 2

The Kingdom of God

The Kingdom of God proclaimed by Jesus is one of justice, peace, and love. Cooperating with God's building of His Kingdom on earth is not an easy task. It means that Christians must always be willing to let God change them, so that they can change the world around them. To encourage them, Christians have God's promise that one day there will be "new heavens and a new earth, where there will be only goodness". (2 Peter 3:13)

What is the Kingdom of God?

A biblical term referring to the reign of God that comes about when God's love and justice come into the world and God's will is carried out by God, recognized and accepted.

Where does the Kingdom of God exist?

Both in the present, in the hearts of people who live Jesus' Law of Love, and in the future when God will draw all things together fully in Christ.

Where is the Kingdom of God seen in the present?

In acts of love, peace, and justice—not in the desire for earthly power.

What are Christians called to do?

To cooperate with God's building His Kingdom on earth through the power of the Holy Spirit.

Why isn't God's Kingdom a complete reality on earth now?

Because people reject God's call to holiness and choose instead to act in selfish, unloving ways.

How can we help in God's building of His Kingdom on earth?

By loving God and by sharing our gifts from God with others, by helping the poor and the oppressed, and by living lives rooted in justice and love, as Jesus calls us to do.

How can we come to better understand the Kingdom of God?

By studying the Beatitudes, which reveal the values that underlie God's Kingdom and serve as guidelines for happy and holy living.

Section 3

Scripture

The Hebrew Bible is the Holy Book of Jews and Christians, and the Bible is the Holy Book of Christians. It has a very long history. It did not come to be all at once. Before many of the materials in the Bible were written, they were passed on by word of mouth. Stories, poems, songs, accounts of events, and prayers were memorized and retold, long before they were put on paper. This way of passing on God's Word is called *oral tradition*. (*Oral* means "spoken.") Christians and Jews believe that God inspired the writing of the Bible to make Himself known to people. Through the Bible, God helps us to understand who God is, what God has in store for creation, and what God asks of people in return.

What is Scripture?

Scripture, or the Bible, is the written record of God's saving acts in history.

What does the word *Scripture* mean?

Scripture means "writing."

What does the Bible contain?

A collection of writings accepted by Christians as being inspired by God and as having divine authority.

What is *inspiration*?

The influence and guidance of God on the writers of the Bible.

What do we mean when we say that the Bible is inspired?

We mean that God made use of the biblical authors' natural abilities and talents and faith to make known to us what He wanted us to know about Himself.

What is *revelation*?

The process by which God has revealed Himself to His people.

Why is the Bible called revelation?

Because the Bible is a means by which God has chosen to reveal Himself in history.

Into how many parts is the Bible divided?

Two parts, the Hebrew Scriptures (Old Testament) and the New Testament.

What does the word *testament* mean?

Testament means "agreement."

Hebrew Scriptures or Old Testament

What are the Hebrew Scriptures?

That part of the Bible, also called the Old Testament, that tells of God's love for and His saving actions among His chosen people, the Jews.

Who is called the first Father (patriarch) of the Jewish people?

Abraham

What did God promise to Abraham?

That He would make of Abraham's descendants a great people with whom He would make an everlasting covenant.

How many books make up the Old Testament?

Forty–six

How are the books of the Old Testament divided?

Into three divisions: the Law, the Prophets, and the Writings.

What is the Pentateuch?

The first five books of the Old Testament, also called the Law or the Torah.

What is the Book of Genesis?

The first book of the Hebrew Scriptures (or Old Testament).

What is the main theme of the biblical story of creation in the Book of Genesis?

That life originally began through God's creative power.

What is the Book of Exodus?

The second book of the Old Testament, which tells how God led the Israelites, the descendants of Abraham, from slavery to freedom.

Who were the twelve tribes of Israel?

Descendants of the grandson of Abraham, Jacob, whom God gave the name *Israel*. Each of Jacob's twelve sons headed a family tribe. These tribes and their descendants were called the twelve tribes of Israel.

What two Old Testament events especially show God's willingness to bring people from slavery to freedom?

Passover and Exodus

To whom did God reveal His divine plan to save His Chosen People?

To Moses

Who is Moses?

The Hebrew leader whom God chose to lead the Israelites out of Egypt and to whom God gave the Ten Commandments.

What is the Decalogue?

The Ten Commandments.

What name for Himself did God give to Moses?

Yahweh, meaning "I Am Who Am."

Why is it important that God revealed His name to Moses?

By telling Moses His name, God showed His desire to establish a more personal relationship with people.

When God revealed Himself to Moses in the Burning Bush, why couldn't Moses look at Him?

Because the power and splendor of God made Moses feel completely unworthy.

What is the great sign of God's love for the Hebrew people?

The covenant God made with Israel on Mt. Sinai.

What is a covenant?

In Old Testament times, a solemn ritual agreement that served as a contract.

What was the covenant Yahweh formed with the Israelites?

That He would be their God and they would be His people.

What is Mount Sinai?

According to the Bible, the place where Yahweh made His covenant with the Israelites, His Chosen People.

What is Passover?

The most important of Jewish feasts, which is celebrated in remembrance of how God delivered the Israelites out of slavery in Egypt to the freedom of the Promised Land.

What is manna?

The special food that God gave the Israelites while they journeyed in the desert on their way to the Promised Land.

What is the Seder Meal?

The annual Jewish ritual meal that commemorates the Lord's saving actions among the Jewish people—the Passover and the Exodus—and the Lord's promise to always be with His people.

Whom did God send to speak in His name when the Israelites were falling into sin?

The prophets

What is a prophet?

A person, divinely inspired, who speaks and acts in the name of God.

What is the job of a prophet?

To remind God's people of God's love and of their responsibilities in terms of the covenant.

What did the prophets often speak out against?

Idolatry and injustices to the poor and oppressed.

What did God promise through the prophets?

That He would send a Savior.

What was the Promised Land?

The land of freedom from oppression that God promised to Abraham.

What is the Babylonian Captivity?

A period of seventy years of enforced exile for the Jewish people. After their revolt against the Babylonian king, all but a few Jews were deported from their own land and taken into captivity in Babylon.

What do "The Writings" consist of?

Those books in the Old Testament that contain collected wise sayings, drama, songs, and fictional stories. They are sometimes called Wisdom Literature. They include Psalms, Proverbs, Song of Songs, Lamentations, and Ecclesiastes.

Who was the greatest of Jewish kings?

David is considered both the greatest Jewish king and the author of some of the Psalms.

What are the Psalms?

Sacred songs or poetic prayers found in the Old Testament.

New Testament

What is the New Testament?

That part of the Bible which is the record of God's love and saving actions in Jesus.

How many books make up the New Testament?

Twenty–seven books.

How is the New Testament divided?

Into four parts: the Gospels, the Acts of the Apostles, the Epistles, and the Book of Revelation.

What are the Gospels?

Four reports of the message and meaning of Jesus.

What does the word *Gospel* mean?

Gospel means "Good News."

What do we call the writers of the Gospels?

Evangelists

What are the names given in the Bible for the evangelists?

Matthew, Mark, Luke, and John.

What is the emphasis of Matthew's Gospel?

That Jesus is the Messiah.

What is the emphasis of Mark's Gospel?

That Jesus is both Messiah and the Son of God.

What is the emphasis of Luke's Gospel?

That Jesus came to save all God's people, Jew and non-Jew.

What is the emphasis of John's Gospel?

That Jesus is God's Word made flesh.

What are parables?

Short stories told by Jesus in the Gospel that help us understand important truths.

Why did Jesus use parables?

To help us better understand God's Kingdom of love.

What parable helps us see God as a forgiving Father?

The parable of the Prodigal Son (also called the parable of the Forgiving Father and the parable of the Unforgiving Brother. (Luke 15:11–32)

What is one parable that helps us to understand what "love of neighbor" means?

The parable of the Good Samaritan. (Luke 10:25–37)

What New Testament passage tells us that Jesus reveals the Father to us?

"Whoever has seen me has seen the Father." (John 14:9)

What story in the Gospels tells us that God watches over each one of us?

The story of the "Good Shepherd."

What are the Epistles?

Letters written by early Church leaders to the people of Christian communities.

How many Epistles are there in the New Testament?

Twenty-one

What are the Acts of the Apostles?

An account of how the Church began and spread during its first years.

What is the Book of Revelation?

The Book of Revelation is the last book of the Bible which presents in symbolic language the final struggle between good and evil.

What does the Church believe about the Bible?

The Church believes that the Bible is God's revelation to His people.

How does the Church protect God's Word from distortion?

By interpreting the Word faithfully, proclaiming it in its liturgy, and using it in its teaching.

Why is God's Word important to us?

Because God is important.

How should Christians respond to God's Word?

By listening to God's Word and by living God's Word.

Is God's Word powerful?

Yes, God's Word is powerful, and Jesus is the most powerful, perfect Word of God.

Section 4

The Catholic Church

The New Testament gives us many ways to think about the Church. We call these ways of describing the Church "images." These images include: Family of God; People of God; Body of Christ; Pilgrim Church; Community of Believers; Social Institution; and the Church as Servant. Together these images describe the essence of the Church.

What is the Church?

The Church is a mystery through which God is present in and through a community of people who believe, accept, and affirm that Jesus is Lord.

Who is the head of the Church?

Jesus Christ

When was the Church established?

On Pentecost, when Jesus gave the fullness of the Holy Spirit to the apostles.

Who were the apostles?

Twelve followers of Jesus chosen by him to lead his Church: Peter, Andrew, James, John, Philip, Bartholomew, Matthew, Thomas, James, Thaddeus (or Jude), Simon, and Matthias (elected to replace Judas).

Who was the apostle to the Gentiles?

St. Paul

What is the Church's source of life?

The Holy Spirit.

Where are the effects of the Holy Spirit seen in the Church?

In the Word of God, in the sacraments, in Church authority, and in the goodness of the Church and its members.

Who belongs to the Catholic Church?

Those who believe in Jesus, have been baptized in his name, and accept the pope as head of Christ's Church on earth and the bishops as successors to the apostles.

What does it mean to be a Catholic?

To be Catholic means sharing in one faith, professing
one Creed, and celebrating seven same sacraments,
under the leadership of the pope and bishops.

What is the central belief of Catholics?

That Jesus Christ is the Son of God, the second Person
of the Blessed Trinity, who became a human being in
order to save people from sin and death.

Why did Jesus send the Holy Spirit to the Church?

So that Jesus' saving work on earth might be continued
throughout time.

**Who does Jesus call to carry out the work of the
Church?**

All the Church's members guided by its bishops and
priests.

How is Jesus with his Church today?

Jesus is with his Church by the power of the Holy
Spirit whom he sent.

**How does Jesus continue to show His saving love
today?**

By the power of the Holy Spirit dwelling in and acting
through Christ's Church.

**Why is each member of the Church important to the
Church's life?**

Because each person is a unique reflection of God and
has special gifts and talents to share with the Church.

How do Catholics express their beliefs?

Through common doctrines, common forms of worship,
and common moral practices.

Why do Catholics come together at Sunday Eucharist?

To praise and thank God our Father in Jesus' name, and to share in the Church's faith, love, and worship.

Why do Christians celebrate the Sabbath on Sunday?

Because that is the day on which, according to Scripture, Jesus rose from death to life.

How is God's Word in Jesus spoken today?

By the power of the Holy Spirit dwelling in the Church.

What are the marks of the Church?

Four qualities that describe the Church.

What are the four marks of the Church?

One, holy, catholic, and apostolic.

What do we mean when we say the Church is one?

We mean that it is a community brought together by faith in one Lord, Jesus.

What is ecumenism?

The movement, inspired by the Holy Spirit, toward unity among Christians.

What do we mean when we say the Church is holy?

We mean it is a community set apart for God, made holy by Jesus.

Is the Church perfectly holy?

The Church on earth, while marked by true holiness, is not perfectly holy. The Pilgrim Church will attain full perfection only in the glory of heaven when it reaches the end of its journey.

What do we mean when we say the Church is catholic?

We mean that it is a community open to all, welcoming all.

What does the word *catholic* mean?

Catholic means "universal."

What do we mean when we say that the Church is apostolic?

We mean it is a community that continues the preaching, teaching, and authority of the apostles.

What are some of the models, or images, of the Church?

Family of God; Body of Christ; Pilgrim People; Servant; People of God; Institution.

Why do we call the Church the *Family of God?*

Because, through Baptism, we are all children of God and brothers and sisters of Jesus Christ.

What does St. Paul compare the Church to?

To the Body of Christ.

Why do we call the Church the *Body of Christ?*

We call the Church the Body of Christ because Christ is its head and we are its members. Like a body, the Church has many parts, but all the parts form one body in Christ.

Why do we call the Church a *Pilgrim People?*

Because like a pilgrim traveling to a holy place, the Church is a people on its way to God and to fullness of life in God's Kingdom.

Why do we call the Church *servant?*

Because the Church's role in the world is to serve, especially to serve the needs of the poor and oppressed.

How does the Church fulfill its role as servant?

By reaching out in justice and love to all human beings who are in need.

Why is the Church committed to social justice?

Because the poor and oppressed will not be fully served until the injustices from which they suffer are done away with.

Why do we call the Church the *people of God?*

Because a people is a community of persons who share something together and act together. The Church community shares belief in Jesus and acts together when it prays and celebrates the sacraments, listens to God's Word, and serves the community's needs.

Why is the Church called a social institution?

Because it is a visible organization dedicated to a particular mission among people.

Why is the Church called a divine institution?

Since it is willed by God, the Church is a divine institution.

What is the Church's mission?

The Church's mission is to bring the message of Jesus Christ to all people.

Leadership in the Catholic Church

Who is the model for Christian leaders?

Jesus, who showed the role of a Christian leader when he washed his disciples' feet.

Who is the head of the Catholic Church?

Jesus Christ is the head of the Church.

Who was the head of the Church on earth after Jesus returned to the Father?

Saint Peter

Who is the pope?

The pope is the successor of Peter, the Bishop of Rome, and the visible head of the Church on earth.

What are some of the pope's titles?

Vicar of Christ (*vicar* means "representative") and Servant of the Servants of God.

What is the papacy?

The office of the pope, who is head of the Church.

What is infallibility?

A gift given to the universal Church which means that by the power of the Holy Spirit, Christ works within the Church in such a way that it does not make a mistake in teaching and believing God's revelation for our salvation. Infallibility means that the Church's faith is not in error.

What is the magisterium?

In the broadest sense, the teaching authority of the whole Church. In the strictest sense, the teaching authority of the Church as embodied in the College of Bishops in union with the pope; or as embodied in the pope.

What is the extraordinary magisterium of the Church?

The College of Bishops teaching by an ecumenical council; or else the pope teaching "ex cathedra" (i.e., "from the chair" of Peter).

When does the pope teach "ex cathedra," that is, as the infallible head of the Church?

When he teaches under these four conditions:

• when he teaches as visible head of the Church (that is, on behalf of the bishops and all believers, more clearly expressing a teaching that the Church already holds);

• when his teaching is intended for all Catholics;

• when he teaches on matters of faith or morality;

• and when he intends to use his full authority to speak infallibly.

What is the Church's structure?

From the earliest days, the Church's structure was organized around people with different degrees of leadership. We call such a structure a *hierarchy*.

What is a hierarchy?

A type of leadership structure in which succeeding ranks have greater authority.

What is a cardinal?

An honorary title given usually to a bishop who serves the Church in a significant way.

What especially important responsibility has been given to cardinals?

The election of a pope.

What are some other important responsibilities of cardinals?

Some important offices which serve the pope in the Vatican and important dioceses are headed by a cardinal.

Who are the Church's ordained leaders?

Its bishops, priests, and deacons.

What is a bishop?

An ordained minister who belongs to the College of Bishops, heads a diocese, and has the power to confer Holy Orders.

How do bishops serve the Church?

As leaders of the universal Church, as members of the College of Bishops, and also as leaders of large regional Churches called *dioceses*.

What is the College of Bishops?

The name given to all bishops who as a group and in union with the pope are supreme authority in the Church. They exercise that authority most clearly during an ecumenical council. The pope by himself is also the supreme authority in the Church.

What is a diocese?

A group of Catholic parishes joined together under the leadership of a bishop.

Who are the bishops' ordained helpers?

Priests and deacons

What is a pastor?

A priest appointed to lead and care for the people in a parish.

What is a parish?

A worshiping community of Catholics established as a unit of the Church under the leadership of a priest.

What is a priest?

A man empowered through the Sacrament of Holy Orders to act in the person of Christ.

How do priests serve the Church?

By proclaiming the Gospel, celebrating the sacraments, and ministering to the spiritual and other needs of the people.

What is a deacon?

An ordained local leader who assists the priests and bishop.

How do deacons serve the Church?

By baptizing, assisting at Mass, preaching, sometimes officiating at weddings and funerals, and by working for social justice and performing various specialized ministries.

Who are members of religious communities?

People who dedicate their lives to prayer and to special work of the Church, live in communities, and profess vows of poverty, chastity, and obedience.

Church Year

What is the Church year?

The Church year, or liturgical year, is an annual cycle of seasons and celebrations that honor and celebrate the mystery of Christ.

How do Catholics honor and remember the special events of Jesus' life?

By celebrating the events of Jesus' life throughout the Church year.

What are the seasons of the Church year?

Advent, Christmas, Lent, Easter Triduum, Easter, and Ordinary Time.

Advent Season

What is Advent?

The season of the Church year when we prepare to celebrate the mystery of Christ's coming at Christmas and at the end of time.

What does the word *Advent* mean?

Advent means "coming."

What does the Church remember during Advent?

That Jesus is always coming into our lives.

Christmas Season

What is the Christmas Season?

> The season during the Church year when we celebrate the birth of Jesus, God's greatest gift to us.

What do Christians remember at Christmas?

> That God's Son, Jesus, was born a human being and that he is with us today.

When does the Christmas Season end?

> The Sunday after the Feast of the Epiphany or after January 6 inclusive.

What does the solemnity of Epiphany especially celebrate?

> The Church's belief that Jesus came for all people, Jews and non-Jews.

Lenten Season

Which Church season is a special time of prayer, penance, and works of love?

> Lent

What is Lent?

> The season when we prepare to celebrate the mystery of Jesus' death and resurrection and deepen the conversion symbolized and begun in our Baptism.

When does Lent start?

> On Ash Wednesday.

What are ashes a sign of?

They remind us that we will die and be held
accountable by God for our lives; they also symbolize
the call from God for us to give up our sins through the
power of Jesus' death and resurrection.

During Lent, what are Christians called to do?

To remember their baptismal promises, to change their
ways, and to return in love to the Father.

How can we prepare ourselves during Lent to do what God asks of us?

We can prepare ourselves through prayer, fasting, and
penance.

What is a Lenten penance?

An act by which a person shows sorrow for and
repentance for sin—offenses against God; an act of
conversion and love made possible by the Holy Spirit.

What does the season of Lent remind us of?

That we are called to live up to our Baptism, which
signifies that Jesus suffered and died that we might
have new life in him.

How long does Lent last?

Lent begins on Ash Wednesday and ends before the
evening Mass of the Lord's Supper on Holy Thursday.

Easter Triduum

What is the Paschal Mystery?

The name given to the saving death and resurrection of
Jesus.

When do we celebrate the Paschal Mystery?

It is celebrated most intensely in the Easter Triduum, but also in all Masses and sacraments.

What is the Easter Triduum?

The most important three days of the Church year when Christians celebrate God's saving acts in Jesus—his Last Supper, his suffering and death, and his resurrection.

How long is the Easter Triduum?

From evening Mass of the Lord's Supper to Easter Sunday evening prayer.

What does the Church celebrate on Holy Thursday?

The Last Supper, the institution of the Eucharist, and the institution of Holy Orders.

What gifts did Jesus share with his apostles at the Last Supper?

The Eucharistic bread and wine; his sacramental Body and Blood.

How do we know that Jesus wanted his followers to remember and repeat what he did at the Last Supper?

Jesus said, " Do this in memory of me." (Luke 22:19)

What does the Mass of the Lord's Supper commemorate?

The special meal that Jesus shared with his friends on the night before he died. The Last Supper was the first Mass.

What does the Church celebrate on Good Friday?

The saving death of the Lord.

How did Jesus die?

He was nailed to a cross upon which he died.

What does the Church celebrate on Holy Saturday?

The Easter Vigil, Jesus' passover from death to life.

What does the Church celebrate on Easter Sunday?

The resurrection of the Lord.

Easter Season

What is the Easter Season?

The season during the Church year when Christians continue to celebrate in the Resurrection, Ascension, and Pentecost the mystery of God's gift of new life to Jesus and to us.

What do Christians celebrate at Easter?

Jesus' passover from death to new life.

When did Jesus rise to new life as he promised he would?

On Easter morning

What other major feasts or solemnities are celebrated during the Easter Season besides the Resurrection?

The Ascension of Jesus and Pentecost.

What do we celebrate on Ascension Thursday?

Jesus' return to his heavenly Father.

What do we celebrate on the feast of Pentecost?

Jesus' sending of the Holy Spirit.

What special word of praise do we use during the Easter Season?

Alleluia is the Easter word of praise.

Ordinary Time

What is Ordinary Time?

That time during the Church year when we celebrate our growth in the Holy Spirit and in being followers of Jesus.

What are some major solemnities that are celebrated during Ordinary Time?

Corpus Christi and the Kingship of Christ.

What do we celebrate in a special way on the solemnity of Corpus Christi?

Jesus' presence with his Church in the Sacrament of the Eucharist.

What do we celebrate on the solemnity of Christ the King?

Jesus as Lord of all.

Section 5

Liturgy and Sacraments

Liturgy is a very important part of being a Catholic Christian. To be Catholic includes sharing in the faith and worship of the Church. We share in the worship of the Church by participating in the weekly celebration of the Eucharist and by celebrating the sacraments, which bring us into closer relationship with Jesus and strengthen us as we follow his way.

What is liturgy?

The Church's official public worship of God.

Do all Catholics follow the same liturgical tradition within the Church?

No. All Catholics profess the same faith, celebrate the same seven sacraments, and acknowledge the pope as visible head of the Church. However, Western Catholics who follow the Roman Rite differ in their liturgical tradition from Catholics who follow one of a number of Eastern Rites.

What is a Rite?

A Rite is a particular tradition, or style of living Christianity, which involves a distinct approach to theology, spirituality, liturgy, and Church law.

What is the major Rite of the Western Church?

The Latin, or Roman Rite.

What are the major Rites of the Eastern Church?

The major Rites of the Eastern Catholic Churches are the Byzantine, Chaldean, Alexandrian, and Armenian Rites.

What does liturgy include?

The celebration of the Eucharist, the celebration of the other sacraments, and the Liturgy of the Hours.

What does the liturgy celebrate?

Christ present and active in his Church.

What is the Church's central act of worship?

The Eucharist

What is one main way we can meet Jesus today?

In the sacraments.

What is a sacrament?

A sacrament is a sacred sign, a symbol which makes Christ present.

What are the most important sacred signs in the Church?

The seven sacraments.

What is the nature of the seven sacraments?

The sacraments are the Church's seven signs of grace through which Jesus continues his saving actions among people and deepens and strengthens our union with God.

What are the names of the seven sacraments?

Baptism, Confirmation, Eucharist, Reconciliation, Anointing of the Sick, Marriage, and Holy Orders.

How do the sacraments enable us to share in Jesus' own life?

By causing what they signify—union with Christ.

What does God offer us through the sacraments?

The gift of grace.

What is grace?

God's divine life within us, the life of the Trinity.

What does grace do?

Grace makes us holy.

Is grace something we can earn?

No, grace cannot be earned; it is a gift from God.

How do we respond to the sacraments?

By freely receiving them with thankful hearts and living out their meaning in our daily lives.

How are the seven sacraments grouped?

Into the Sacraments of Initiation, the Sacraments of Healing, and the Sacraments of Commitment or Service.

What are the Sacraments of Initiation?

Baptism, Confirmation, and Eucharist.

Why are Baptism, Confirmation, and Eucharist called the Sacraments of Initiation?

Because through Baptism, Confirmation, and Eucharist people come to fullness of membership in Christ's Church.

What are the Sacraments of Healing?

Reconciliation and Anointing of the Sick.

What are the Sacraments of Service?

Matrimony and Holy Orders.

Sacrament of Baptism

When did you become a member of God's family, the Church?

At Baptism

What is Baptism?

A sacrament through which those who believe in Jesus become members of his Body, the Church, and receive a share in divine life.

What do we become through Baptism?

Brothers and sisters of Christ, heirs of God, and sharers in Christ's priesthood.

How do we share the priesthood of Jesus?

By worship and prayer in union with Jesus.

In whose name are we baptized?

We are baptized in the name of the Father, and of the Son, and of the Holy Spirit.

Who is the ordinary minister of Baptism?

A priest is the ordinary minister of Baptism, but in extraordinary situations any person may baptize.

What does the priest use when he baptizes someone?

Water (the sign of new life) and oil.

What does the priest say when he baptizes?

The priest says, "I baptize you in the name of the Father, and of the Son, and of the Holy Spirit."

What does the priest do when he baptizes?

The priest pours water three times over the head of the person being baptized while saying the words of baptism; he draws a cross on his or her forehead with holy oil; he places a white garment or stole over the person and gives him or her a candle.

Why is a candle given at Baptism?

The candle is a sign of the light of God's love within us. It reflects the light of the Easter Candle, just as we are to do.

What does the white baptismal garment mean?

The garment is a sign that the newly baptized person is a child of God and very special to God and to the Christian family. If a stole is used, it brings out the status of the newly baptized as sharing in the priesthood of Christ.

Sacrament of Confirmation

What is Confirmation?

A sacrament through which those who have been baptized in Christ share more fully in the gifts of the Holy Spirit and in membership in Christ's Church.

What does the Sacrament of Confirmation call us to do?

The Holy Spirit calls and enables us to be witnesses for Christ.

How can we be witnesses to our faith?

By living out and expressing our Catholic faith.

At Confirmation what do we receive and accept?

We receive the strength to accept the challenge to grow as Christians.

What do we renew at Confirmation?

Our baptismal promises.

What do Baptism and Confirmation allow us to share in?

The gifts of the Holy Spirit.

Who is the ordinary minister at Confirmation?

The bishop or priest.

What does the bishop use to confirm?

The bishop or priest uses holy oil called chrism.

What does the bishop do?

The bishop or priest anoints the candidate with oil.

What does the bishop or priest say?

The priest or bishop says, "Be sealed with the gift of the Holy Spirit."

Sacrament of the Eucharist

What is the Sacrament of the Eucharist?

The Church's central act of worship through which we are more deeply united with Jesus and his Church.

How is the Eucharist best described?

As both a sacred meal and a sacrifice.

What does the word *Eucharist* mean?

Eucharist means "thanksgiving."

How can the Church best offer thanks to God for all His gifts?

Through its celebration of the sacraments, especially the Eucharist.

What is the Mass?

Another name for the celebration by the Catholic Church of the Sacrament of the Eucharist.

What are the four basic parts of the Mass?

Introductory Rites, Liturgy of the Word, Liturgy of the Eucharist, and Concluding Rites.

What do the Introductory Rites of the Mass include?

Entrance Song or Antiphon, Greeting, Penitential Rite, Kyrie (Lord, have mercy), Song of Praise, and Opening Prayer.

During what part of the Mass do we confess our sorrow for sin?

During the Penitential Rite.

What is the Liturgy of the Word?

That part of the Mass during which we listen to readings from the Bible and respond with reflection and prayer.

What does the Liturgy of the Word include?

Reading from the Old or New Testament, Psalm Response, Reading from the New Testament, Gospel Acclamation, Gospel, Homily, Creed, and General Intercessions.

What is the homily?

Teaching given by the priest during the Mass based on the Word of God.

What is the Liturgy of the Eucharist?

That part of the Mass which is a special prayer of praise and thanks to God during which Christ becomes sacramentally present for our offering to God and for our Communion.

What does the Liturgy of the Eucharist include?

Preparation of Gifts, Prayer over the Gifts, Eucharistic Prayer, The Our Father, Sign of Peace, Lamb of God, Communion Rite, and Prayer after Communion.

What does the Concluding Rite consist of?

The Blessing and Dismissal.

What gifts do we offer God at Mass in thanksgiving for all that He has given us?

Gifts of bread and wine.

What do the gifts of bread and wine represent?

The bread and wine represent ourselves and become Christ sacramentally present, presented to God and presented to us.

What is the name of the special prayer of praise and thanks that we offer through Christ to the Father at Mass in the power of the Holy Spirit?

The Eucharistic Prayer.

What prayer at Mass helps us remember that we belong to God's one family?

The Lord's Prayer

What happens to the bread and wine offered at Mass?

The bread and wine become the sacramental Body and Blood of Jesus.

What do we call the special way in which Jesus comes to us at Mass?

Holy Communion

What do we share when we receive Holy Communion?

The Body and Blood of Christ.

What do we show by receiving Holy Communion?

That we want to be one with God in Christ, to follow Jesus, and to be part of his Body, the Church.

What do we say when we receive Jesus in Holy Communion after the priest, deacon, or Eucharistic minister says,"The Body of Christ"?

We say "Amen."

What does the word *Amen* mean?

Amen means "Yes, it is really so."

What part of the Mass particularly makes us into and reminds us that we are one Body in Christ?

Holy Communion

What do we say at the end of Mass?

We say, "Thanks be to God."

Why do we say "Thanks be to God" at the end of the Mass?

To thank God for the love He has shown us in Jesus.

What does the Church want us to do after we leave Mass?

To share God's love by loving and serving others.

Does the Mass end when we leave church?

No, we should carry the Mass into our lives by praying, loving, and serving one another.

When did Jesus give us the gift of the Eucharist?

At the Last Supper.

What is the Catholic Christian Passover celebration?

The Eucharist

What sacrament is a sign of God's wanting to draw people into closer unity with the Trinity?

The Eucharist

Sacrament of Reconciliation

What is the Sacrament of Reconciliation?

A sacrament through which Christ offers forgiveness of sins to us sinners. We can accept this forgiveness by being truly sorry for our sins.

What does the word *reconciliation* mean?

Reconciliation means "bringing together again."

What special words does the priest say to bring God's forgiveness to us sacramentally?

"I absolve you from your sins in the name of the Father, and of the Son, and of the Holy Spirit."

What does the priest do to show that God has forgiven us?

The priest extends his hands over the penitent and pronounces the words of forgiveness.

What do we call this action?

Absolution

What are the four essential parts of Reconciliation?

Contrition, confession, absolution, and acceptance of penance.

What is penance?

An act that serves as a sign of a penitent's willingness to accept God's forgiveness and to change his or her life.

Why do Catholics confess their sins to a priest?

The priest acts as a representative of Christ and his Church and has the power to bring forgiveness from God and the Church.

What three ways can the Sacrament of Reconciliation be celebrated?

Individually, communally with individual absolution, or communally with general absolution.

How often will God forgive us?

As often as we are truly sorry for our sins and ask for His forgiveness.

Anointing of the Sick

What is Anointing of the Sick?

A sacrament through which Christ offers the healing, strengthening powers of the Holy Spirit to those who are sick and suffering and his consolation to those who are dying.

Who receives the Sacrament of Anointing?

People of all ages who suffer from sickness, the ill effects of old age, or who are dying.

What does the anointing show people?

That the Church cares about them and that God's healing, saving power is available.

What can those who suffer show the Church community?

How to bear suffering well, in union with the suffering of Jesus.

What does the priest use for anointing?

The priest uses blessed oil to anoint the forehead and palms of the hands.

What other sacraments are often received along with Anointing?

Reconciliation and Eucharist.

Why is the Sacrament of Anointing important to the recipient's family?

They can draw strength and peace of mind from this sign of the Church's caring concern and of God's healing and saving power.

Sacrament of Matrimony

What is Matrimony?

A sacrament through which Christ joins a Christian man and woman in a life-giving, love-giving, lifelong union, which reflects Christ's union with his Church.

Who are the ministers of the Sacrament of Matrimony?

The man and woman who are marrying one another.

What role does the priest play during the celebration of the Sacrament of Matrimony?

The priest represents Christ and the Church; he presides at the ceremony ordinarily and is one of the witnesses.

What does the couple being married do?

The couple makes solemn promises (or vows) to live together as husband and wife.

What does the couple say?

I (name) take you (name) to be my husband/wife. I promise to be true to you in good times and in bad, in sickness and in health. I will love you and honor you all the days of my life. (Rite of Marriage, No. 45)

What is the Nuptial Blessing?

A prayer included in the Rite of Marriage that asks God to look with love upon and to strengthen the couple being married.

Why does the Sacrament of Matrimony ordinarily take place at Mass whenever possible?

Because the Eucharist brings out the full meaning of the other sacraments, including Christ's desire that all might be one and his bringing that about.

What does the wedding Mass represent?

The couple's sacrifice of thanksgiving through Jesus in the Spirit to God the Father.

What is the union of husband and wife in Christian marriage a sign of?

The union of Jesus and his Church.

Why does the couple exchange rings?

As a special sign of their commitment to be united and faithful for life.

What is a married couple's unique gift to the Church?

A married couple serves as a sign of Christ's union with the Church.

What is the role of the Christian community at a wedding?

By their attendance at the wedding the community shows that they recognize the couple's love as holy, and they encourage the couple as they promise to be faithful and to love each other forever.

What is the love that is celebrated in the Sacrament of Marriage a model and ideal for?

It is a model and ideal for the love that we are to have for one another as Christians.

Sacrament of Holy Orders

What is Holy Orders?

A sacrament through which Christ ordains and empowers a man to act in the person of Christ as priest.

Who shares the special responsibilities of ordained priesthood?

Bishops, priests, and deacons.

How do the Church's ordained leaders carry on Christ's priesthood?

They preach, teach, celebrate the sacraments, and exercise serving authority in the Church community.

Who is the ordinary minister of Holy Orders?

The bishop

What does the bishop do when he ordains a man to Holy Orders?

The bishop ordains through the laying on of hands.

Why does the bishop place his hands on the head of the priest being ordained?

It is the special sign of the giving of the Holy Spirit and of responsibility to the Church.

What does the priest witness to?

To the presence of the Trinity in the community.

What is the most important job of the priest?

Leading the celebration of the Eucharist, including the preaching of the Gospel.

What does God do through the actions of the priest at the Eucharist?

God transforms bread and wine into the sacramental Body and Blood of Jesus.

Sacramentals

What are sacramentals?

Sacramentals are special signs—words, gestures, objects— that the Church uses to make present and remind us of Christ's love.

What are some sacramentals used by Catholics?

Gestures (Sign of the Cross, Sign of Peace, genuflection), objects (holy water, crucifix, rosary, medals, statues), and words (blessing of objects and individuals, litanies).

What do sacramentals bring and remind us of?

Sacramentals bring and remind us of Christ's love present in the life of the Church.

How should Catholics use sacramentals?

Catholics should use sacramentals with faith and devotion, and never make them objects of superstition or magic.

What is the difference between sacramentals and sacraments?

Sacraments are more important, more central, and more clearly established by Christ. They are also more certain, clear, and effective signs of Christ's presence. Sacramentals are more dependent on our faith and devotion.

Section 6

Morality

Christian morality is human morality raised to the divine dimension. Christian morality involves living in such a way that our lives reflect the values and teaching of Jesus. It means seeing life as a relationship with God and our fellow human beings, and acting out of love for God and people as Jesus did.

What is morality?

Human actions as they affect the good of oneself, of someone else, or of society.

What is Christian morality?

A way of living that reflects the moral values and teachings of Jesus.

Who helps Christians to live a moral life?

The Holy Spirit dwelling within us.

What is immorality?

Human actions that are wrong or sinful.

How do we know if something is moral or immoral?

By listening to our conscience and acting upon it.

What is conscience?

A power given to us by God that enables us to decide whether an act is right or wrong and to make good choices.

Are we born with a rightly formed conscience?

Our conscience forms as we grow and learn from experience.

What is a rightly formed conscience?

A conscience formed by listening to God's Word in Scripture, to the teaching of the Church, and to the inspiration of the Spirit within us.

Must every Catholic have a rightly formed conscience?

Yes, every Catholic is obliged to develop a rightly formed conscience.

What must we know for our conscience to be rightly formed?

We must know what our responsibilities are as Christians.

How can we learn what our responsibilities as Christians are?

By listening to God's Word in Scripture, in prayer, in the experiences of human life, and in the teachings of the Church.

What does following your conscience mean?

It means to do what your rightly formed conscience tells you to do.

Who are the Church's official and authentic teachers of Christian life?

The pope and the bishops in communion with the pope.

What responsibilities do Christians have toward God?

Christians are obliged to worship God; to give God first place in their lives; to honor God's name; and to show respect for persons, places, and things related to God.

What responsibilities do Christians have toward others?

Christians are obliged to act in justice and charity toward others; to respect and obey lawfully exercised authority; to be concerned about others temporal and spiritual needs; and to express these concerns in action.

What responsibilities do Christians have toward self?

Christians are obliged to become like Christ; to love themselves since Christ loves us; to choose what is morally right; and to avoid sin.

What is a temptation?

An invitation to choose a thought or action that our conscience has determined is wrong.

Is a temptation a sin?

No, a temptation is not a sin; temptation becomes sinful only when it is accepted and carried out.

What should we do in times of temptation?

We should call upon God in prayer to help us reject the temptation. (II Corinthians 12:9)

When we are faced with a moral decision, what should we do?

1. Pray, asking God for guidance;
2. listen to what our conscience is saying, which includes what it is hearing in the Bible, Church teaching, and the wisdom of the human community;
3. do what our conscience tells us is right.

Guidelines for Moral Living

To what does God call all people?

To holiness; to union with God.

What does God want us to become?

The best persons we can be.

How do we become the best persons we can be?

By practicing virtue.

What is virtue?

Habitual action that promotes the good of the individual or of society.

What are the three theological (pertaining to God) virtues?

Faith, hope, and charity.

What are the four most important moral virtues?

Justice, temperance (moderation), fortitude (courage), and prudence (wise action).

What are the cardinal virtues?

Another name for the most important moral virtues. *Cardinal* means "key."

What is the virtue of justice?

The moral virtue that enables us to give to others what is due to them as a matter of right—to be fair in dealing with others.

What is the virtue of temperance?

The moral virtue that enables people to control the desires of the senses and to use them according to the will of God.

What is the virtue of fortitude?

The moral virtue that gives us the strength and endurance to bear suffering and to undertake difficult tasks for the purpose of accomplishing good.

What is the virtue of prudence?

The moral virtue that enables us to judge rightly and to make good decisions.

How can good moral habits be developed?

By recognizing our sinful tendencies and then developing the virtues that will help overcome them; by recognizing what are good actions for us to do and then developing the habit of doing them.

What is the greatest of all virtues?

Charity or love

Rules the Church Lives By

What are the greatest Commandments?

"Love the Lord your God with all your heart, with all your soul, with all your strength, with all your mind; and love your neighbor as you love yourself." (Luke 10:27)

What is Jesus' Law of Love?

"Love one another just as I love you." (John 15:12)

How will people know that we are Jesus' disciples?

Jesus said, "If you love one another, then everyone will know that you are my disciples." (John 13:35)

What laws, norms, and guidelines tell us how to love God and our neighbor?

The Ten Commandments, the Beatitudes, the Laws of the Church, the Corporal Works of Mercy, and the Spiritual Works of Mercy.

What are the Ten Commandments?

Ten rules for living in response to God's love; they were part of God's covenant made with the Israelites on Mt. Sinai.

1. I, the Lord, am your God. You shall not have other gods besides Me.

2. You shall not take the name of the Lord, your god, in vain.

3. Remember to keep holy the Sabbath day.

4. Honor your father and your mother.

5. You shall not kill.

6. You shall not commit adultery.

7. You shall not steal.

8. You shall not bear false witness against your neighbor.

9. You shall not covet your neighbor's wife.

10. You shall not covet anything that belongs to your neighbor.

(National Catechetical Directory, Appendix A)

What are the Beatitudes?

Jesus' guidelines for happy and holy living for those who seek God's Kingdom; they were given by Jesus in the Sermon on the Mount.

Blessed are the poor in spirit;

for theirs is the kingdom of heaven.

Blessed are the meek;

for they shall possess the land.

Blessed are they that mourn;

for they shall be comforted.

Blessed are they who hunger and thirst after justice;

for they shall have their fill.

Blessed are the merciful;

for they shall obtain mercy.

Blessed are the pure of heart;

for they shall see God.

Blessed are the peacemakers;

for they shall be called the children of God.

Blessed are they that suffer persecution for justice's sake;

for theirs is the kingdom of heaven.

(Matthew 5:3–10)

What are the Laws of the Church?

Specific duties that Catholic Christians are expected to fulfill.

1. To keep Sundays holy; and to participate in Mass on Sunday and holy days of obligation.
2. To lead a sacramental life, frequently receiving the Eucharist.
3. To prepare for Confirmation and to be confirmed.
4. To observe the marriage laws of the Church and to provide children with religious training.
5. To strengthen and support the Church.
6. To do penance, including abstaining from meat and fasting from food on appointed days.
7. To join in the missionary spirit and works of the Church.

(Adapted from *Concise Catholic Dictionary for Parents and Religion teachers* by Reynolds Ekstrom and Rosemary Ekstrom)

What are the Corporal Works of Mercy?

Human actions motivated by love of God and neighbor, relating to the bodily needs of others.

1. Feed the hungry
2. Give drink to the thirsty

3. Clothe the naked
4. Visit the imprisoned
5. Shelter the homeless
6. Visit the sick
7. Bury the dead.

What are the Spiritual Works of Mercy?

Seven charitable works encouraged by the Church related to the spiritual well-being of others.

1. Convert sinners
2. Instruct the ignorant
3. Counsel the doubtful
4. Comfort the sorrowful
5. Bear wrongs patiently
6. Forgive all injuries
7. Pray for the living and the dead.

What do the Works of Mercy mean to the Church?

The Works of Mercy show that the Spirit is at work in the Church carrying on Jesus' mission.

When do we reach spiritual maturity?

Reaching spiritual maturity is a lifelong process.

Sin

What is sin?

Sin is freely choosing to do what we know is wrong.

How do we sin?

By freely choosing to do something that we know God does not want us to do.

What is Original Sin?

The sin of the first human beings, which is found in all human beings, and to which we say yes by our personal sins. It is fundamentally and formally overcome by Baptism and, for adults, the repentance connected with Baptism.

What is personal sin?

Evil that we ourselves freely choose.

What is social sin?

Evil that is brought about by the way a society is organized or functions. (Racism, for example, is social sin.)

When do people sin?

When they knowingly and freely act in selfish and unloving ways, contrary to God's will.

Are some sins more serious than others?

Yes, some sins are more serious than others.

What do we call very serious sin?

Mortal sin

What is mortal sin?

Sin that destroys our friendship with God.

What do we call sin that is not mortal sin?

Venial sin

What is venial sin?

Sin that weakens or takes away from our friendship with God but does not destroy it.

What four questions should we ask ourselves to determine whether or not an act is sinful?

1. Does it go against the Ten Commandments, the Beatitudes, Jesus' Law of Love, or the laws of the Church?

2. How serious are the results of what I choose to do?

3. Am I choosing freely?

4. Does my conscience tell me that the act is right or wrong?

What seven attitudes lead to most sins?

Pride, greed, envy, gluttony (addiction), lust, anger, and sloth (laziness).

What are these attitudes called?

The capital sins.

Even though we sin, will God forgive us?

Yes, God will always forgive us if we are truly sorry for our sin.

Why should we forgive others?

We should forgive others because God forgives us and because Jesus tells us to forgive.

Section 7

Prayer

Prayer is response to the presence of God. Prayer deepens our friendship with God and helps us want to do God's will. Scripture tells us that Jesus prayed often. Sometimes he spent whole nights alone in prayer to his Father. Sometimes he prayed with others, often using the Psalms—the formal prayers of the Jews. The Psalms of the Old Testament are fine examples of prayer, expressing the hopes, fears and dreams of the Jewish people.

What is prayer?

Communication with God; it is speaking with and listening to God.

Why should Christians pray?

Because prayer is a way of returning praise and thanks to God for all God has given us.

What are the four purposes of prayer?

1. Adoration (to worship)
2. Thanksgiving (to thank)
3. Sorrow (to say, "I'm sorry")
4. Petition (to ask).

What special sign in God's name do Catholics pray?

The Sign of the Cross: In the name of the Father, and of the Son, and of the Holy Spirit. Amen.

Which prayer tells what Christians believe?

The Creed

What are the names of two forms of the creed that Catholics use?

The Apostles' Creed and the Nicene Creed.

Which creed is used during Mass?

The Nicene Creed

What prayer did Jesus teach us?

The Lord's Prayer

What prayer helps us remember that we are all God's children?

The Lord's Prayer

Is there only one way to pray?

No, there are many kinds of prayer.

What are some forms of prayer?

Formal prayer, spontaneous prayer, personal prayer, meditation, contemplation, shared prayer, liturgical prayer.

What is formal prayer?

Prayers that contain a set form of words and that many people know (such as, the Our Father and the Hail Mary).

What is spontaneous prayer?

Prayer that persons make up by themselves at the moment.

What is personal prayer?

The private prayer of an individual.

What is meditation?

A form of mental prayer involving reflection on God or a religious truth.

What is contemplation?

A form of mental prayer that involves being aware of God's presence and rejoicing in it.

What is shared prayer?

Spontaneous prayer and/or formal prayer within a group.

What is liturgical prayer?

The official public prayer of the Church, including the Rites of all the sacraments and the Liturgy of the Hours.

What is the Church's most important prayer?

The Eucharist

What is devotional prayer?

Group or private prayer that centers around and honors God, Christ, Mary, or the saints in a particular way.

What are some forms of devotional prayer?

The rosary, stations of the cross, forty hours, novenas.

What is the rosary?

A form of devotional prayer honoring Mary, which consists of using a string of beads while saying Our Fathers, Hail Marys, and Glory to the Fathers.

Can our whole life be a prayer?

Yes, if prayer is living in awareness of the presence of God. Jesus showed us that such prayer is possible.

Section 8

Mary and the Saints

Saints were people just like us. They weren't perfect, but they lived their lives in such a way that they reflected God's perfect image in a bright and wonderful way. The lives of the saints show forth the beauty and glory of God. Their lives stand as an example of what our lives can be.

Who are saints?

Members of the Church whose lives were Christ-like in a particularly outstanding way and who have been proclaimed saints by the Church.

Who is greatest of the Church's saints?

Mary, Mother of Jesus.

Who is Mary?

Mary is the mother of God's Son, Jesus.

Through whose power was Jesus born of Mary?

Through the power of the Holy Spirit.

Why does the Church honor Mary?

Because she is the Mother of Jesus and Mother of the Church.

What does Mary call herself?

Servant of the Lord.

What does Mary show us by her life?

By her life, Mary shows us how to faithfully respond to God's call to holiness.

What is Mary's special prayer called?

The Hail Mary

What is Mary's prayer of praise called?

The Magnificat (Luke 1:46–55)

What are the three major Marian feasts celebrated during the Church year?

The Solemnity of Mary, Mother of God (January 1); The Solemnity of the Assumption of Mary (August 15); and the Solemnity of the Immaculate Conception (December 8).

When does the Church celebrate Mary's birthday?

On September 8.

What does *solemnity* mean?

A feast of greatest rank.

What does *memorial* mean?

A feast of least rank.

What does the Assumption celebrate?

Mary being taken up to heaven.

What does the Solemnity of the Immaculate Conception commemorate?

The Church's belief that Mary was sinless or filled with grace from the very first moment of her life.

What do Catholics call the feast that celebrates Mary's visit to her cousin, Elizabeth?

The Visitation

Under what title is Mary honored as Patroness of the Americas?

Under the title of "Our Lady of Guadalupe."

Who was the husband of Mary and the guardian of Jesus?

St. Joseph

Under what title does the Church honor St. Joseph?

St. Joseph, Patron of the Universal Church.

What is the communion of saints?

The union of all the people of God, both living and dead, with Christ and each other.

Why are the lives of the saints important?

The lives of the saints reflect Jesus present and active in the Church through the power of the Holy Spirit.

What do the saints' lives show us?

That God calls each of us, in our own way, to special friendship with Him and service to God's people.

What do the lives of the saints remind us of?

The lives of the saints remind us that we can be holy, too.

What is canonization?

The process through which a person is declared a saint in the Catholic Church.

What is beatification?

One of the official steps in the canonization process; the person who is beatified is called "blessed."

What is All Saints' Day?

The day the Church honors all who have died and who share full union with God.

What does All Saints' Day remind us of?

That God is calling people to union with Himself and with one another in and through Jesus Christ.

When is All Saints' Day?

November 1

What is a patron saint?

A saint who is held in special honor by a certain person or group.

What is the Litany of the Saints?

A prayer in which we call on the saints to pray for us.

What is a martyr?

A saint who has suffered death because of his or her faith.

What does the word *martyr* mean?

Martyr means "witness."

Section 9

Death and Eternal Life

Jesus tells us, "I am the resurrection and the life. Whoever believes in me will live even though he dies; and whoever lives and believes in me will never die." (John 11:25) Jesus' death and resurrection make it possible for us to share in his promise of new life forever. We remember Jesus' promise every time we pray the Creed, "On the third day he rose again. . . ." Our lives must show this belief.

What do Christians believe about death?

Christians believe that for those who are in Christ death is a passage to eternal life.

Was death the end for Jesus?

No, Jesus rose to new life through the power of God.

What sign do Christians have that God gives life after death?

Jesus' death and resurrection.

Why did God raise Jesus from the dead?

So that death would not have power over Jesus and that in and through Jesus people could share eternal life.

What is redemption?

Jesus' saving us from sin and death by his suffering, death, and resurrection.

What did Jesus promise to those who believe in him?

New life forever.

What is eternal life?

The state of fully sharing in God's life forever after a person passes through the experience of death.

What did Jesus say to Martha about eternal life?

"I am the Resurrection and the Life. Whoever believes in me will live even though he dies; and whoever lives and believes in me will never die." (John 11:25)

What did Jesus teach us about death?

That at death life is not taken away, it is changed.

What is purgatory?

A state of purification through which some of the people of God pass after death and before they experience heaven.

Should we pray for those who have died?

The Church teaches that it is a "very excellent and noble" work to pray for all who have died, except for official saints (we pray *to* them, not *for* them).

On what day does the Church pray in a special way for all who have died?

On November 2, the Feast of All Souls.

What is heaven?

The name Christians give to sharing fully in the life of God after death.

Is heaven a place?

No, it is a state of existence in which we will enjoy eternal happiness in God's presence forever.

What is hell?

Hell is the name Christians give to a state of eternal rejection of God.

What does the pain of hell consist in?

The pain of hell consists in the frustration, suffering, and deep loneliness of having cut oneself off from God, the source of joy and happiness; it consists of the pain we have inflicted on ourselves.

Did Jesus speak of hell?

Jesus warned that those who reject God will be cut off from God in eternity. (e.g., Matthew 18:6–9)

Can any person know who goes to hell?

Only God knows who is in hell, if anyone. Whether or not a person is in mortal sin is beyond anyone's ability to judge.

What do Christian funeral rites involve?

The celebration of the Eucharistic liturgy for a Christian who has died.

What does the funeral liturgy include?

It includes our coming to terms with our sorrow, especially in the wake service, our uniting our prayers with Christ in the Eucharistic celebration of Jesus' saving death and resurrection, and our handing over of the person to God in hope, finalized in the Burial Rite. We celebrate the hope of resurrection in Christ.

What parable shows us how we will be judged at the end of time?

The parable of The Final Judgment. (Matthew 25:31–46)

In the parable of The Final Judgment, what does the King tell those whom he welcomes into God's Kingdom?

Whatsoever you did for the least of my brothers and sisters, you did for me. (See Matthew 25:40)

Section 10

Appendix

Catholic Dictionary

Abraham—The first of the patriarchs called by God; called "Father" by all who worship the God of Abraham.

Absolution—The freeing from sin by God, through the priest, in the Sacrament of Reconciliation.

Abstinence—To refrain from an act, such as eating, and offering the action to God.

Acolyte—A person who serves the deacon or priest at liturgical celebrations.

Acts of the Apostles—A New Testament book that tells the story of the early Church.

A.D.—Abbreviation for years occurring after the approximate time of Christ's birth.

Adultery—Sexual intercourse by a married person with someone other than his or her spouse.

Advent—A season during the Church year when the Church prepares for the birth of Jesus and Jesus' coming at the end of time.

Agnostic—A person who claims ignorance of whether God exists.

All Saints' Day—A holy day of obligation on which the Church honors its saints, celebrated November 1.

All Souls' Day—The day the Church remembers and prays for those who are being purified for heaven; celebrated November 2.

Alleluia—Hebrew word meaning "Praise God" or "Praise the Lord."

Almsgiving—Giving money, food, or clothing to help the less fortunate.

Amen—Word meaning, "Yes, it is really so."

Angels—Spiritual beings who have understanding and free will; often used by God as messengers.

Annulment—The declaration by the Church that a marriage did not exist.

Annunciation—Solemnity celebrating the angel's announcement to Mary of her conception of Jesus by the power of the Holy Spirit; celebrated March 25.

Anoint—To rub with oil.

Anointing of the Sick—A sacrament through which Christ offers the healing, strengthening powers of the Holy Spirit to those who are sick and suffering, and his consolation to those who are dying.

Anointing with Oil—An external sign used in the Sacraments of Baptism, Confirmation, Holy Orders, and Anointing of the Sick.

Apocalypse—The Book of Revelation in the New Testament.

Apostasy—Rejection of one's faith.

Apostles—The title given to men Jesus called to be leaders of his Church.

Apostles' Creed—A profession of faith, which is a summary of the truths that the apostles taught.

Apostolic—Relating to the apostles and their time in history.

Apparition—An appearance by Jesus, Mary, saints, or angels to individuals or groups.

Archbishop—Usually, the bishop of an archdiocese.

Ark—The special box in which the Ten Commandments were carried.

Ascension—Solemnity recalling Jesus' return to the Father forty days after the resurrection.

Ash Wednesday—First day of Lent; a day of fast and abstinence.

Ashes—The remains of burned palms from the previous year's Palm Sunday; used to mark people's foreheads with the Sign of the Cross on Ash Wednesday.

Assumption—Solemnity celebrating Mary's being taken into heaven.

Atheist—A person who believes that there is no God.

Atonement—Doing penance for sins one has committed.

B.C.—Abbreviation for the years before Christ's birth.

B.C.E.—Abbreviation meaning "Before the Common Era"; the common era is the era common to people of various faiths, Christians, Jews, and Muslims, and so forth, the years after the birth of Christ.

Babylonian Exile—The period of time during which most of the Jewish people were taken into captivity in Babylon, approximately 587 to 537 B.C.

Baptism—A sacrament through which those who believe in Jesus become members of his Body, the Church, receive new life in the power of the Holy Spirit, and the promise of life forever with the Trinity.

Beatification—One of the final steps in the canonization process. The person who is beatified is called "Blessed."

Beatitudes—The standards for a happy life given by Jesus in his Sermon on the Mount.

Benignity—Kindness, one of the fruits of the Holy Spirit.

Bible—The Holy Book of Christians; the written record of God's saving acts in history.

Blasphemy—The use of profanity or insulting words when referring to God and His Church.

Body of Christ—An image of the Church in which the Mystical Union of Christ (the head) and his followers (the members) is compared to the unity of the human body.

Book of Revelation—Last book of the Bible; presents in symbolic language the final struggle between good and evil.

Breath of Yahweh—Biblical term interpreted by Christians as referring to the Holy Spirit.

Calumny—Lies that hurt the reputation of another person.

Capital Sins—Seven attitudes that can lead to sin; sometimes called the cardinal sins: pride, covetousness, lust, anger, gluttony, envy, and sloth.

Cardinal—An honorary title usually bestowed on a bishop who has served or is serving the Church in a significant way; most cardinals serve as electors of a new pope; many head important dioceses or offices in the Vatican.

Cardinal Virtues—Another name for the moral virtues: justice, temperance, fortitude, and prudence.

Celibacy—The state of not being married and abstaining from sexual intercourse.

Centering Prayer—A type of prayer in which a person turns all of his or her concentration inward and ultimately to God.

Chalice—A cup to hold the sacred wine used at the Eucharist.

Chancellor—A person appointed by a bishop to supervise certain administrative affairs of a diocese as outlined in canon law.

Chaplain—Priest appointed to pastoral service in an institution, hospital, military, or religious community.

Character—The moral qualities of a person.

Charity—A virtue combining the qualities of love, benevolence, and good will; kindliness and generosity toward others. One of the theological virtues.

Chastity—A virtue that helps direct a person's sexuality toward correct use.

Chasuble—Flowing outer garment worn by the priest at Mass.

Chi-Rho—Greek symbol for Christ.

Chosen People—The term applied to the Jewish people signifying that they were chosen by God for a special covenant.

Chrism—Mixture of olive oil and balsam blessed by the bishop on Holy Thursday and used primarily in the celebration of the Sacraments of Confirmation, Holy Orders, and Anointing of the Sick.

Christians—Followers of Jesus.

Christmas—The solemnity and season of the Church year when the Church celebrates the birth of Jesus.

Church—Union of all those who believe in Jesus, follow his way, and are united in him.

Church Year—Liturgical cycle of seasons and feasts celebrating the mystery of Christ.

Ciborium—A special cup that holds the Eucharistic Bread at Mass and in the tabernacle.

Code of Canon Law—Rules that state the rights and duties of Church members and help the Church operate for the common good.

College of Cardinals—All of the cardinals in the Church.

Commandment—Law of God.

Communal Penance—Services at which the community joins in prayer before and after private confession, or sometimes without private confession.

Communion of Saints—The union of all people, living and dead, who belong to the family of God.

Community—A group of people united by common beliefs, values, tasks, and responsibilities.

Concelebration—A celebration of Eucharist in which more than one priest, led by one of the group, preside at Mass together.

Confession—Telling our sins to a priest in the Sacrament of Reconciliation.

Confirmation—A sacrament through which those who have been baptized in Christ share more fully in the gifts of the Holy Spirit and in membership in Christ's Church.

Conscience—The capability given to us by God to make good choices.

Consecration—The part of the Mass during which the priest, using the words of Jesus, changes the bread and wine into the sacramental Body and Blood of Christ.

Contrition—The state of repentance, being sorry.

Convent—Residence of women religious.

Corporal—Square linen cloth on the altar during Mass on which to place the chalice and ciborium.

Corporal Works of Mercy—Human actions, motivated by love of God and neighbor, relating to the bodily needs of others.

Corpus Christi—Solemnity in honor of the Eucharist; a Latin word meaning "Body of Christ."

Counsel—The gift of the Holy Spirit through which we receive the Spirit's guidance in practical matters.

Covenant—A solemn ritual agreement between two parties.

Covet—To enviously desire what belongs to someone else.

Creed—A prayer telling what the Church believes.

Cremation—The burning of human remains.

Crosier—A staff; the insignia of the office of bishop.

Crucifix—A cross on which there is the image of Jesus crucified.

Cruets—Small pitchers that hold the water and wine used at the Eucharist.

Curse—Wishing evil upon a person.

David—Greatest king of Israel; author of some of the Psalms in the Bible.

Decalogue—Ten Commandments.

Dehumanize—Take away or lessen the dignity or basic rights of another.

Despair—To refuse to trust in God; or the state of refusing to do so.

Detraction—Damaging a person's reputation by unnecessarily revealing his or her faults.

Devotions—Pious practices done to honor God or the saints; generally including formal prayers, such as novenas, or actions, such as wearing a medal or scapular.

Diaconate—The order received prior to ordination to the priesthood (transitional diaconate); or with the intent to remain a deacon and not become a priest (permanent diaconate).

Diocese—Territorial jurisdiction of a bishop.

Disciples—Followers of Jesus.

Dispensation—Exemption from a rule or law by a person in authority.

Divine Life—The life of God, grace.

Divine Praises—A litany of praise recited after Benediction of the Blessed Sacrament.

Divorce—The supposed civil dissolution of a marriage.

Doctrine—Term referring to important teachings of the Church.

Dogma—A doctrine officially and most solemnly declared by the Church.

Easter—The solemnity and season of the Church year when Christians celebrate Jesus' rising from death to new life.

Easter Triduum—The Church liturgical season which consists of the holiest days of the Church year: from Thursday evening to Sunday evening of Holy Week.

Ecumenical Council—An assembly of all of the Catholic bishops called by the pope for the purpose of formulating official Church teaching and practice.

Ecumenism—The effort of all Christian Churches to work toward full unity among all Christian peoples.

Edifying—Uplifting morally and spiritually by good example.

Elizabeth—Mary's cousin and mother of John the Baptizer.

Encyclical—Pastoral letter addressed by a pope to the whole Church.

Epistles—Letters to the first Christian communities, which are part of Scripture.

Eternity—Life after our physical death; God's life.

Ethical—In accordance with moral standards for right conduct.

Eucharist—A sacrament which is the Church's central act of worship and through which Catholic Christians are more deeply united with Jesus Christ, and through Jesus with his Church; the word *Eucharist* means "thankfulness."

Eucharistic Flagon—A bottle or large pitcher that holds the Eucharistic Wine, which is to be poured into chalices for distribution at Masses where Holy Communion is given out in both forms.

Eucharistic Plate—A special plate which holds the Eucharistic Bread to be distributed at Mass.

Eucharistic Prayer—A prayer of thanksgiving, commemoration, and consecration used by the priest during the Liturgy of the Eucharist.

Euthanasia—Killing or unjustifiably permitting the death of those who are ill or dying; mercy killing.

Evangelist—Someone who brings good news; title commonly given to the writers of the four Gospels.

Evangelization—The process of proclaiming the Gospel.

Ex Cathedra—The expression used for the times the pope speaks infallibly; it means "from the chair (of Peter)."

Excommunicate—To separate a person from community with the Church.

Exegesis—Interpretation of the Scriptures.

Exodus—A book of the Old Testament containing the story of how God led the Israelites, under the leadership of Moses, from slavery in Egypt to freedom in the Promised Land; or the liberation itself.

Exorcism—To drive out evil spirits through the power of the Holy Spirit in the name of Jesus.

Faith—To believe in God and the truths revealed by God; one of the theological virtues; "to be sure of the things we hope for, to be certain of the things we cannot see" (Hebrews 11:1).

Faithful—Practicing members of the Church—"the faithful."

Fast—To take no food or liquids, or a limited amount, during a prescribed period of time.

Fear of the Lord—Great love and reverence for the Lord.

Fervent—Having great devotion.

Fidelity—The quality of being loyal and faithful.

Forgiveness—Being set free from sin and guilt.

Formal Prayer—Prayers that contain a set form of words and that many people know.

Fornication—Sexual intercourse between unmarried persons.

Fortitude—Courage in facing hardship for what is right; one of the cardinal moral virtues.

Forty Hours Devotion—Exposition of the Blessed Sacrament for forty hours, during which the Church community spends time in prayer and meditation.

Free Will—The ability to choose between alternatives.

Fruits of the Spirit—Love, joy, peace, patience, kindness, goodness, faithfulness, humility, and self-control. (Galatians 5:22–23)

Fundamentalist—One who believes in only a literal interpretation of the Bible.

General Absolution—The form of sacramental forgiveness given when individual confession is not done, for example, because it is not possible.

Genesis—First book of the Bible.

Genuflection—A brief kneeling on the right knee as a sign of respect when the Blessed Sacrament is present in the tabernacle.

Gifts of the Spirit—Special powers of the Spirit bestowed on the Church and all its members to enable them to carry out Jesus' mission: wisdom, understanding, counsel, fortitude, knowledge, piety, and fear of the Lord.

Gluttony—Overeating or overdrinking; one of the capital sins.

Good Friday—The day on which Jesus was crucified and died.

Gospels—Four reports of Jesus' life, death, and resurrection.

Grace—God's life within us.

Guardian Angel—Special angel assigned to guide and inspire us and to keep us from evil.

Hail Mary—Prayer in praise of Mary, asking for her intercession.

Healing—Restoration to health.

Hebrew Scriptures—The first part of the Bible, also called the Old Testament or Hebrew Bible, that tells of God's love for and His saving actions among His Chosen People.

Hebrews—A name referring to the Jewish people, particularly before their Exodus from Egypt.

Hell—The state of eternal rejection of God.

Heresy—Denial of a truth of the Catholic faith.

Hierarchy—Leadership in the Catholic Church.

Holy—Sacred or set apart for God.

Holy Communion—The sacramental Body and Blood of Christ in which Catholic Christians are united more deeply with Jesus and with the Church.

Holy Days of Obligation—Days on which Catholics are required to participate in the Mass.

Holy Orders—A sacrament through which Christ through a bishop ordains and empowers a man to act in the person of Christ as bishop, priest, or deacon.

Holy Saturday—Saturday of the Triduum, when the Easter Vigil is celebrated.

Holy See—The root of Church authority in Rome, under the leadership of the pope.

Holy Spirit—Third Person of the Blessed Trinity; the Spirit of Love.

Holy Thursday—The first day of the Triduum, which commemorates the Last Supper when Jesus gave us the gift of the Eucharist and instituted Holy Orders.

Homily—A talk given by the priest or deacon during a liturgical celebration on the Word of God.

Hope—The theological virtue that helps us trust in God and His promise of eternal life.

Host—Used to refer to the bread used at Mass, both before and after the consecration.

Human Rights—Freedom and dignity basic to all individuals.

Humanism—A system of thinking about human existence using the dignity, value, and worth of human beings as its base.

Humanitarian—A person concerned with advancing the welfare and social justice of others.

Humility—Quality which enables people to see themselves as they are and to acknowledge their limitations.

Idolatry—Worshiping any creature or thing in place of God.

Immaculate Conception—Solemnity, of December 8, celebrating the belief that Mary was without sin from the first moment of her existence.

Immortality—Eternal life won by Jesus through his suffering, death, and resurrection as a possibility offered to all people.

Incarnation—The doctrine that the second Person of the Blessed Trinity took human form as Jesus Christ and that Jesus is both God and human.

Indulgence—Remission of temporal punishment due for sins; a partial indulgence does away with part of the consequences of sin, and a plenary indulgence does away with all of the consequences of sin.

Infallibility—A characteristic of the Church which enables the pope or the bishops in union with the pope to teach without error on matters of faith or morals.

Infancy Narratives—Scripture stories of Jesus' birth and infancy.

Inspiration—The influence and guidance of God on the authors of the Bible.

Integrity—The human quality that involves not only knowing what is right or wrong, but choosing to do what is right.

Intercession—Prayer of petition.

Irreverence—Lack of respect for someone or something sacred.

Israelites—Descendants of Jacob; the people whom God delivered out of Egypt and with whom God made a covenant on Mt. Sinai.

Jeremiah—A prophet of God.

Jerusalem—The city sacred to Jews.

Jesus' Law of Love—The words of Jesus that sum up all of God's laws: "Love one another just as I love you."

Jesus' Public Life—The three years or less during which Jesus taught and preached among the people.

Jewish People—God's Chosen People; used to refer to the Israelites after the Babylonian Exile.

John the Baptizer—A prophet who called people to make ready the way of the Lord.

Joseph—Foster father of Jesus.

Justice—Giving to people what is rightfully theirs; one of the cardinal moral virtues.

Kingdom of God—The reign of God; everyone can cooperate with God's building of His kingdom by doing God's will.

Laity—Members of the Church who are not ordained.

Lamb of God—New Testament name for Jesus, which emphasizes his obedient sacrafice of love to the Father for us.

Last Supper—The meal that Jesus shared with his apostles on the night before he died and during which he gave the gift of the Eucharist.

Lectern—The reading stand used in Church.

Lectionary—The book of Scripture from which the priest and lector read at Mass.

Lector—The person who reads the first two Scripture readings at Sunday Mass or the first reading at weekday Mass.

Lent—That time during the Church year when Catholic Christians prepare to celebrate the mystery of Jesus' death and resurrection, and a time when they recall and deepen their baptismal promises especially by practicing penance.

Limbo—A term used in the past in an attempt to explain the eternal destiny of unbaptized children who died; also used for the place or state where the souls of all the just rested until heaven was reopened by Jesus.

Liturgical Year—The Church's yearly cycle of seasons and feasts which celebrate the mystery of Christ.

Liturgy—The official public worship of the Church.

Lord's Prayer—Prayer that Jesus taught, as recorded in Scripture; the Our Father.

Lust—The desire for unlawful bodily pleasure; one of the capital sins.

Madonna—Another title of respect for Mary, which literally means "my Lady."

Magisterium—The teaching authority of the Church.

Magnificat—Mary's prayer of praise, recorded in Luke 1:46–55.

Manifestation—A "showing" or "revealing" that can easily be perceived by the senses.

Manna—The special food God gave to the Israelites in the desert.

Marian Theology—Teachings and traditions of the Church regarding Mary, Mother of God.

Martyr—Someone who dies for his or her faith.

Mary—Mother of Jesus and Mother of the Church.

Mass—The name Catholics give to the celebration of the Sacrament of the Eucharist.

Matrimony—A sacrament through which Christ joins a Christian woman and man in a life-giving, love-giving, lifelong union, reflecting Christ's union with his Church.

Mediator—A person who stands between two parties in order to bring them together.

Messiah—The Savior God promised in the Hebrew Scriptures.

Ministry—Service in or to the Church.

Miracle—An extraordinary event showing God's intervention in human affairs.

Miter—Hat worn by bishops at liturgical functions.

Modesty—A virtue that helps a person have moral restraint in words, actions, and dress in sexual matters.

Monastery—Residence for a community of monks or nuns.

Monk—Religious priest or brother who lives in a monastic community.

Monotheism—Belief in one God.

Monsignor—An honorary title bestowed upon those who have been chosen for papal recognition because of their services to the Church.

Monstrance—Gold case used for the exposition of the Blessed Sacrament.

Mortal Sin—Serious sin that destroys our friendship with God.

Moses—The leader of God's Chosen People who led them from slavery to freedom and to whom Scripture tells us that God gave the Ten Commandments.

Mount Sinai—The place where Scripture tells us that God made an everlasting covenant with the Jewish people.

Mysteries—Events whose meanings we will never completely understand.

Nave—Main body of a church building.

New Testament—The written record of God's saving actions in Jesus and the Church.

Nondivine existence—Life lived apart from God; sin.

Novena—Devotional prayers, often to Mary or one of the saints, repeated for nine days or one day a week for nine weeks.

Novitiate—Period of formal training and formation of a man or woman preparing for membership in a religious community.

Nun—A woman who belongs to a religious order who has made solemn vows.

Nuptial Blessing—A prayer included in the Rite of Marriage that asks God to look with love upon and to strengthen the couple being married.

Nuptial Mass—Mass at which a marriage is celebrated.

Oath—Asking God to witness the truth of what one says or pledges.

Obligation—Duties imposed by the laws of God, the Church, or moral law.

Occasion of Sin—Any person, place, or thing that is a temptation to sin for a particular person.

Oral Tradition—Accounts of events passed from generation to generation by word of mouth.

Ordinary Time—That time during the Church year when Catholic Christians celebrate growth in the Holy Spirit and in being followers of Jesus.

Ordination—Rite through which men enter the ordained ministry.

Ordo—Book of directions for the Mass and Divine Office on a daily, yearly basis.

Original Sin—The state of imperfection and evil into which human beings are born, because of the disobedience of Adam and Eve.

Pagan—A person who does not believe in the God of Abraham, Isaac, and Jacob; a person who is not a Christian or a Jew.

Papal Mass—Eucharistic celebration at which the pope presides.

Parable—A short story that helps us understand a truth.

Parish—Territorial community of the faithful, usually, centered in a Church building.

Parish Council—Parish leadership body to which members are elected, appointed, or else serve on because of their office (e.g., pastor or staff member); they help lead the parish.

Paschal Mystery—A term referring to Jesus' passover from death on the cross to the new life of the resurrection.

Passion Sunday—The last Sunday in Lent, recalling Jesus' triumphant entry into Jerusalem and his suffering (passion) and death. Passion Sunday has been traditionally called Palm Sunday.

Passover—Celebration and remembrance of the Jewish passover from slavery in Egypt to freedom and new life in the Promised Land.

Pastor—An ordained priest charged with the responsibility of a parish, or a bishop of the diocese.

Pastoral Letter—A letter written by a bishop, or bishops, to Church members.

Paten—Flat dish used to hold the large host (Eucharistic bread) at Mass or to catch particles of hosts during distribution of the Eucharist.

Patriarch—The early leaders of the Hebrew people; *patriarch* means "father."

Pectoral Cross—Cross on a chain worn by a bishop or an abbot as a sign of office.

Penance—An act that shows we are sorry for our sins and are willing to change our lives.

Pentateuch—The first five books of the Bible: Genesis, Exodus, Leviticus, Numbers, and Deuteronomy.

Pentecost—Christian feast celebrated fifty days after Jesus' resurrection to remember the outpouring of the Holy Spirit upon Jesus' first followers.

People of God—The Church.

Permanent Diaconate—The first of the major orders of the Sacrament of Holy Orders when it is received with the intent to remain a deacon and not become a priest.

Perseverance—The continuation of a course of action despite difficulties.

Personal Sin—Freely choosing to do what one knows is wrong.

Peter—One of Jesus' original twelve apostles who was the leader of the Christian community after the Ascension of Jesus; the first pope.

Pharisee—A member of an influential Jewish group some of whom interpreted the Mosaic Law strictly and others less strictly.

Pilgrimage—Prayerful journey to a place of devotion.

Poor Box—Collection box for the less fortunate.

Pope—Successor to Peter, the Bishop of Rome, and the visible head of the Church on earth.

Prayer—Communication with and awareness of God.

Precepts of the Church—Seven Church laws governing Catholics.

Prejudice—Having preconceived opinions about someone or something without knowing all of the facts.

Prelate—Priest of high rank; usually, a bishop or cardinal.

Presentation—The feast on which Catholics remember and honor the presentation of the infant Jesus in the temple at Jerusalem by Mary and Joseph, celebrated February 2.

Pride—Believing that we are, and desiring to be treated as though we are, more important than we are; one of the capital sins.

Priest—A man empowered through the Sacrament of Holy Orders to proclaim the Gospel, celebrate the sacraments, lead the people, and minister to the spiritual needs of the people.

Priesthood—Being one of those who have been authorized to offer acts of worship to God; the second of the major orders of the Sacrament of Holy Orders.

Prophecy—Divine revelation given by God through a person God inspired.

Prophets—Persons God chooses to speak in His name.

Providential—Pertaining to divine providence; coming from, or seeming to come from, God.

Prudence—A virtue that helps us make practical decisions and judgments; one of the cardinal moral virtues.

Psalm—A sacred song or poem.

Psalms—The book of hymn prayers in the Old Testament.

Purgatory—State of purification through which some pass after death and before they experience heaven.

Real Presence—Jesus' presence in the Sacrament of the Eucharist under the appearances of bread and wine.

Reconciliation—A sacrament through which Christ forgives the sins of those who are truly sorry by means of the priest's absolution; *reconciliation* means "to bring together again."

Reconciliation Room—Small room used for the celebration of the Sacrament of Reconciliation.

Rectory—Residence for priests.

Redemption—The process by which humanity was returned to God's life of grace and freed from sin through the life, death, and resurrection of Jesus Christ.

Redemptive Suffering—Pain or distress that is patiently endured and offered up to God in union with Christ for the forgiveness of one's own, or someone else's, sins.

Reign of God—Another name for "Kingdom of God"; the power and love of God.

Relic—Part of the bodily remains of a saint or items associated with the saint's life, such as clothing.

Religious—A man or woman who belongs to a community and who takes the vows of that community, ordinarily including poverty, chastity, and obedience.

Reparation—To make amends for a wrong a person has done.

Responsibility—Duties for which one is held accountable.

Restitution—Payment for damage or injury to another person or a person's property; returning lost or stolen property.

Resurrection—Jesus' passover from death to life in and through the power of God.

Retreat—A time set aside to renew or deepen one's relationship with God through a series of religious exercises and religious services.

Revelation—What God reveals to His people and the process by which God does so.

Rite—The words and actions used in Church ceremonies; also a particular tradition, or style of living Christianity, which involves a distinct approach to theology, spirituality, liturgy, and Church law (e.g., Byzantine Rite).

**Rite of Christian Initiation
of Adults**—The process by which adults are formally
brought into Christ and the Church.

Roman Curia—Body of officially organized agencies that
assist the pope in governing and
administering the Church.

Rosary—A form of devotional prayer honoring and praying
to Mary.

Sacramentals—Special signs—words, gestures,
objects—that the Church uses to bring and
remind us of Christ's love.

Sacramentary—Book the priest uses that contains the
order of the Mass, that is, the prayers to
be used that day and every day.

Sacraments—The Church's seven signs of grace through
which Jesus continues his saving actions
among people and that deepen and
strengthen our union with God.

Sacraments of Healing—Reconciliation and Anointing of
the Sick; sacraments which bring
Christ's healing to us.

Sacraments of Initiation—Baptism, Confirmation, and
Eucharist; the sacraments by
which a person is initiated into
the Catholic Church.

Sacraments of Service—Holy Orders and Matrimony;
sacraments of commitment.

Sacrarium—Special sink for washing the sacred vessels
used at Mass.

Sacrifice—The offering of a gift to God.

Sacrificial Giving—Pledging a percentage of one's income
to the support of the Church and to
the support of those in need.

Sacrificial Lamb—An animal offering given to God that represented the people's willingness to offer themselves to God and to be one with Him.

Sacrilege—Lack of respect and mistreatment of sacred persons, places, or things, or the reception of the sacraments unworthily.

Sacristan—Person who takes care of the sanctuary, sacred vessels, and altar linens.

Sacristy—Room used to store the sacred vessels, vestments, and so forth, in a church.

Saints—People of courage whose lives were Christ-like in a particular way and have been declared saints by the Church.

Salvation—An act through which a person is brought from nondivine existence and sin to freedom from sin, to healing, and, ultimately, to the fullness of divine life in heaven.

Sanctify—To make holy.

Sanctoral Cycle—Feasts of saints celebrated by the Church in the course of a year.

Sanctuary—Portion of the Church that contains the altar.

Sanctuary Lamp—A lamp in the sanctuary that signifies (when lit) that the Body of Christ is in the tabernacle.

Savior—Jesus Christ, who was born, suffered, died, and rose again for the reparation of people's sins, that is, for their salvation.

Schism—A separation in the Church due to a dispute about certain beliefs and/or practices.

Scribe—Member of a professional group who are scholars on God's Law in Israel.

Scripture—Another name for the Bible; the word *Scripture* means "writings."

Seder—The Jewish ritual meal that commemorates the Lord's saving actions among the Jewish people in the Exodus and Passover and the Lord's promise to always be with His people.

Sin—Freely choosing to do what we know is wrong or choosing something other than God or what God asks of us.

Slander—Harming another person's reputation by telling lies or distorting the truth.

Sloth—Laziness

Soul—The spiritual part of a person.

Spirit—The third Person of the Blessed Trinity is called the Holy Spirit; also refers to that which gives life to one's actions and motivates one to act in a certain way.

Spiritual—Nonmaterial; relating to the soul and to one's relationship to God who is completely spiritual or nonmaterial.

Spiritual Works of Mercy—Seven charitable works encouraged by the Church related to the spiritual well-being of others.

Spontaneous Prayer—Prayer that a person creates by himself or herself.

Stations of the Cross—A series of fourteen meditations on the sufferings, death, and burial of Jesus. These scenes are mounted in Catholic Churches and the practice is to move from scene to scene while praying and meditating; some have added a fifteenth station, the resurrection, to bring out more of the Paschal Mystery, especially, its ultimately joyous conclusion.

Sunday—The day of the Lord's resurrection and a time for spiritual renewal.

Supernatural—Beyond the natural order or power of things.

Synagogue—The place where Jews meet to study and worship, aside from the Temple in Jerusalem, when it existed.

Synoptic Gospels—The Gospels of Matthew, Mark, and Luke; the first three Gospels in the New Testament.

Tabernacle—The place where the Eucharistic Bread (and occasionally Wine) are kept.

Temperance—The virtue that enables us to control the desires of the senses and use them according to God's will; one of the cardinal moral virtues.

Temptation—A strong urge to do something we know is wrong.

Ten Commandments—Ten laws, recorded in the Old Testament, that God gave to Moses to help people live holy and happy lives.

Testament—Means "an agreement."

Theology—The field of religious thought about God, His qualities, and His relations to the universe.

Tithing—Giving a portion of one's income for the support of the Church.

Torah—The law governing Jewish life contained in the first five books of the Bible (the Pentateuch); also another name for the Pentateuch .

Tradition—Information, beliefs, and customs which are handed down from one generation to another; the process by which this is done.

Transitional Diaconate—The first of the major orders of the Sacrament of Holy Orders, received prior to ordination to the priesthood.

Transubstantiation—Term used to explain the conversion of the bread and wine into the sacramental Body and Blood of Jesus during Mass.

Trinitarian Life—The life of the Father, Son, and Holy Spirit.

Trinity—Three Persons in one God.

Twelve Tribes—Descendants of the twelve sons of Jacob, who was called Israel; the original tribes of Israel.

Vatican—Residence of the pope; also the location of the officials who assist the pope.

Vatican II—A general ecumenical council, called by Pope John XXIII, during which the pope and the bishops established teaching norms and pastoral guidelines for the Church in its mission of evangelization.

Venerate—To give honor, respect, and admiration.

Venial Sin—Less serious sin that takes away from our friendship with God but does not destroy it.

Vestibule—Foyer and entrance to a Church.

Viaticum—The Sacrament of the Eucharist received by a dying person; strictly speaking, this is the sacrament of the dying.

Vicar of Christ—A title for the pope; *vicar* means "representative."

Vigil—The day before certain feasts, such as Easter; a time of waiting.

Virtue—Habitual actions that promote the good of an individual or of society.

Vocation—Call from God to a particular way of life.

Wisdom—A gift of the Holy Spirit that enables us to judge rightly about the things of God and to desire the things of God rather than the things of the world.

Word of God—Revelation; Christians also call Jesus "the Word of God."

Worship—Love, adoration, and honor that belongs to God alone.

Writings—A name for the Wisdom Books in the Old Testament.

Yahweh—The name for God that God gave to Moses.

Prayers Catholics Should Know

The Lord's Prayer

Our Father, who art in heaven hallowed be thy name.
Thy kingdom come, thy will be done on earth as
it is in heaven. Give us this day our daily bread,
and forgive us our trespasses as we forgive those
who trespass against us. And lead us not into temptation,
but deliver us from evil. Amen.

Hail Mary

Hail, Mary, full of grace, the Lord is with you.
Blessed are you among women, and blessed is the
fruit of your womb, Jesus.

Holy Mary, Mother of God, pray for us sinners,
now and at the hour of our death. Amen.

Trinity Prayer

Glory to the Father, and to the Son,
and to the Holy Spirit.
As it was in the beginning, is now,
and will be, forever. Amen.

Morning Offering

God, my Father, I give you today, all that I think, and do
and say. And I unite with all that was done by Jesus Christ,
your dearest Son.

Grace before Meals

Bless us, O Lord, and these your gifts, which we are about to receive from your bounty, through Christ, our Lord. Amen.

Thanksgiving after Meals

We give you thanks, almighty God, for these and all your blessings, through Christ our Lord. Amen.

Apostles' Creed

I [we] believe in God, the Father
almighty,
creator of heaven and earth.

I [we] believe in Jesus Christ, his only
Son, our Lord.
He was conceived by the power of the
Holy Spirit
and born of the Virgin Mary.
He suffered under Pontius Pilate,
was crucified, died, and was buried.
He descended to the dead.
On the third day he arose again.
He ascended into heaven,
and is seated at the right hand of the
Father.
He will come again to judge the living
and the dead.

I [we] believe in the Holy Spirit,
the holy catholic Church,
the communion of saints,
the forgiveness of sins,
the resurrection of the body,
and the life everlasting. Amen.

Nicene Creed

We believe in one God, the Father, the almighty, maker
of heaven and earth, of all that is seen and unseen.
We believe in one Lord, Jesus Christ, the only Son of
God, eternally begotten of the Father, God from God,
Light from Light, true God from true God, begotten,
not made, one in Being with the Father.
Through him all things were made. For us men and for
our salvation he came down from heaven: by the power of the
Holy Spirit he was born of the Virgin Mary, and became
man.
For our sake he was crucified under Pontius Pilate; he
suffered, died, and was buried.
On the third day, he rose again in fulfillment of the
Scriptures; he ascended into heaven and is seated at
the right hand of the Father.
He will come again in glory to judge the living and
the dead, and his kingdom will have no end.
We believe in the Holy Spirit, the Lord, the giver of
life, who proceeds from the Father and the Son.
With the Father and the Son, he is worshiped and glorified.
He has spoken through the prophets.
We believe in one, holy, catholic, and apostolic Church.
We acknowledge one baptism for the forgiveness of sins.
We look for the resurrection of the dead, and the life of the
world to come. Amen.

Act of Contrition

O my God, I am sorry for my sins. In choosing to sin,
and failing to do good, I have sinned against you and
your Church. I firmly intend, with the help of your
Son, to do penance and to sin no more.

Act of Faith

Lord God, I believe that you are one God in three Persons.
I believe that you are Father, Son, and Holy Spirit.
I believe that a new life opened for me through the death

and resurrection of your Son and that your love and guidance
continue through your Holy Spirit. I believe in the truths
taught by your holy, catholic, and apostolic Church. By
responding in love to your gifts, I believe that I shall
share in eternal joy with you. This is my belief, Lord God,
and my belief is my joy. Amen.

Act of Hope

Lord God, trusting in your deep love and goodness,
I hope to receive continued forgiveness for my faults
and your guidance and help in avoiding sin. My hope for
eternal life and joy with you fills me with joy and
love each day I live. Amen.

Act of Love

Lord God, You continually share your great love with me
through the gifts in my life. In an attempt to imitate
your great goodness and show my love in return, I will
strive to love you with all my heart, all my mind, and
all my strength. And I will seek to love my neighbor as
myself. Lord, teach me to love even more. Amen.

Gloria

Glory to God in the highest,
and peace to his people on earth.
Lord God, heavenly King,
almighty God and Father,
we worship you, we give you thanks,
we praise you for your glory.
Lord Jesus Christ, only Son of the
Father, Lord God, Lamb of God,
you take away the sin of the world:
have mercy on us;
You are seated at the right hand of the
Father: receive our prayer.
For you alone are the Holy One,
you alone are the Lord,

you alone are the Most High,
Jesus Christ, with the Holy Spirit,
in the glory of God the Father. Amen.

Prayer to the Holy Spirit

Come, Holy Spirit, fill the hearts of your faithful,
and kindle in them the fire of your love.
Send forth your Spirit, and they shall be created,
and you shall renew the face of the earth.

Let us pray. God, you teach the hearts of your people
by the light of your Holy Spirit. By the same Spirit,
grant that we may judge all things right, and rejoice
always in his comforting.

The Confiteor

I confess to almighty God, and to you my brothers and
sisters, that I have sinned through my own fault in
my thoughts and in my words, in what I have done and
in what I have failed to do; and I ask the Blessed
Mary, ever Virgin, all the angels and saints and
you, my brothers and sisters, to pray for me to the
Lord our God.

Divine Praises

Blessed be God.
Blessed be his Holy Name.
Blessed be Jesus Christ, true God and true man.
Blessed be the Name of Jesus.
Blessed be his most Sacred Heart.
Blessed be his most Precious Blood.
Blessed be Jesus in the most Holy Sacrament of the Altar.
Blessed be the Holy Spirit, the Paraclete.
Blessed be the great Mother of God, Mary most holy.
Blessed be her holy and immaculate Conception.
Blessed be her glorious Assumption.
Blessed be the name of Mary, Virgin and Mother.

Blessed be St. Joseph, her most chaste spouse.
Blessed be God in his angels and in his saints.

Serenity Prayer

God grant me the serenity to accept the
things I cannot change . . .
Courage to change the things I can, and
Wisdom to know the difference.

Prayer for the Dead

Eternal rest grant unto them, O Lord,
and let perpetual light shine upon them.
May they rest in peace. Amen.

The Memorare

Remember, O most gracious Virgin Mary, that never was it
known that anyone who fled to your protection, implored
your help, or sought your intercession was left unaided.

Inspired by this confidence, I fly unto you, O Virgin
of virgins, my Mother; to thee I come, before thee I
stand, sinful and sorrowful. O Mother of the Word
Incarnate, despise not my petitions, but in your mercy
hear and answer me. Amen. (St. Bernard)

The Magnificat

My soul proclaims the greatness of the Lord, my spirit
rejoices in God my Savior for he has looked with favor
on His lowly servant.
From this day all generations will call me blessed: the
Almighty has done great things for me. His Name is holy;
from one generation to another, he shows mercy to those who
honor him.
He has stretched out his mighty arm and scattered

the proud with all their plans.
He has brought down mighty kings from their thrones
and lifted up the lowly.
He has filled the hungry with good things and sent
the rich away with empty hands.
He has kept the promise he made to our ancestors,
and has come to the help of his servant Israel.
He has remembered to show mercy to Abraham and to
all his descendants forever! (Luke 1:46–55)

Hail, Holy Queen

Hail holy queen, mother of mercy; hail our life, our
sweetness, and our hope! To you do we cry, poor banished
children of Eve. To you do we send up our sighs, mourning
and weeping in this vale of tears. Turn then, most gracious
advocate, your eyes of mercy toward us; and after this our
exile, show unto us the blessed fruit of your womb, Jesus.

The Angelus

The angel of the Lord declared to Mary,
and she conceived of the Holy Spirit.
Hail Mary full of grace . . .
Behold the handmaid of the Lord.
Be it done unto me according to Thy word.
And the Word was made flesh
and dwelt among us.
Hail Mary full of grace . . .
Pray for us, O holy Mother of God.
That we may be made worthy of the promises of Christ.

Let us pray: Pour forth we beseech you, O Lord, your
grace into our hearts that we, to whom the Incarnation
of Christ, your Son, was made known by the message of
an angel, may by his passion and cross be brought to
the glory of his resurrection, through the same Christ
our Lord. Amen.

Prayer to St. Joseph

O Joseph, model of all who labor, pray to God with us.
It is an honor to use the gifts and develop the talents
He has given us. May God's grace strengthen us to work
with order and patience, thankfulness and joy. We pray
that we may strive dutifully and conscientiously to
fulfill our tasks, that all our accomplishments may
benefit others and serve their needs. Then may the Lord
crown our efforts at the hour of death, that we may join
in praising him forever. Amen.

Prayer of St. Francis

Lord, make me an instrument of your peace.
Where there is hatred, let me sow love;
where there is injury, pardon;
where there is doubt, faith;
where there is despair, hope;
where there is darkness, light;
where there is sadness, joy.
Lord, grant that I may not
so much seek to be consoled, as to console;
to be understood, as to understand;
to be loved, as to love.
For it is in giving that we receive;
it is in pardoning that we are pardoned;
and it is in dying that we are born to
eternal life.

Mass Responses

Introductory Rite
Priest: The Lord be with you.
People: And also with you.

Penitential Rite
Priest: Brothers and sisters, to prepare ourselves to
celebrate the sacred mysteries, let us call to mind
our sins.

Priest:	You were called to heal the contrite. Lord, have mercy.
People:	Lord, have mercy.
Priest:	You came to call sinners. Christ have mercy.
People:	Christ, have mercy.
Priest:	You plead for us at the right hand of the Father. Lord have mercy.
People:	Lord, have mercy.
Priest:	May almighty God have merciy on us, forgive us our sins, and bring us to everlasting life.
People:	Amen.

Gospel Response

Priest:	This is the Word of the Lord.
People:	Praise to you, Lord Jesus Christ.

Eucharistic Acclamations

Priest: Let us proclaim the mystery of faith.

A. People: Christ has died,
Christ has risen,
Christ will come again.

B. People: Dying You destroyed our death,
Rising You restored our life,
Lord Jesus, come in glory.

C. People: When we eat this bread, and drink this
cup, we proclaim your death, Lord Jesus,
until you come in glory.

D. People: Lord, by your cross and resurrection
you have set us free.
You are the Savior of the world.

Rite of Communion

Priest: This is the Lamb of God who takes away
the sins of the world. Happy are those who are
called to his supper.

All: Lord, I am not worthy to receive you,
but only say the word and I shall he healed.

Dismissal
Priest: Go in peace to love and serve the Lord.
People: Thanks be to God.

Mysteries of the Rosary

Joyful Mysteries
(Mondays and Thursdays)

1.   The Annunciation
2.   The Visitation
3.   The Nativity
4.   The Presentation
5.   Finding of the child Jesus in the Temple

Sorrowful Mysteries
(Tuesdays and Fridays)

1.   Agony in the Garden
2.   Scourging of Jesus
3.   Crowning of Thorns
4.   Jesus Carries his Cross
5.   The Crucifixtion

Glorious Mysteries
(Sundays, Wednesdays, and Saturdays)

1.   Resurrection of Jesus
2.   Ascension of Jesus
3.   The Descent of the Holy Spirit on the Apostles
4.   Assumption of Mary
5.   Coronation of Mary

Stations of the Cross

1. Jesus is Condemned to Death
2. Jesus Carries His Cross
3. Jesus Falls the First Time
4. Jesus Meets His Mother
5. Simon Helps Jesus Carry His Cross
6. Veronica Wipes the Face of Jesus
7. Jesus Falls the Second Time
8. Jesus Speaks to the Women of Jerusalem
9. Jesus Falls the Third Time
10. Jesus Is Stripped of His Garments
11. Jesus Is Nailed to the Cross
12. Jesus Dies on the Cross
13. Jesus Is Taken Down from the Cross
14. Jesus Is Laid in the Tomb

How to Pray Using Scripture

- Choose a Gospel passage (for example, the Sunday Gospel). Read the passage thoughtfully.
- Replay the Gospel story in your imagination, placing yourself in the story.
- Be aware of how you feel about what is happening. Think about what you would say and do.
- Tell Jesus or the Father how you feel and what you think about the Gospel story.
- Before ending your prayer, thank God for something that your prayer made you aware of.

Examination of Conscience

1. How did I show my love for God and others?
2. Did I usually say my daily prayers?
3. Did I always obey my parents?
4. Did I think of others—my parents, brothers and sisters, friends. Was I mean to them?
5. Was I kind and fair in the way I played and worked?
6. Did I use my body only as God intended?
7. Did I share my things with others?
8. Did I care for my things and the things of others?
9. Did I hurt others by telling lies or by stealing or by calling them names?
10. Did I worship God by going to Mass and taking part in the celebration?

Forms of Prayer

Liturgical prayer is participating in the worship of the Church, in particular, the Eucharist and the sacraments. It is responding to God as a community while God offers Himself to us.

Individual prayer is responding to God as an individual. It is a person's own unique response.

Formal prayer is a response that has been composed by others for persons to use.

Spontaneous prayer is a response in which the person praying uses nonprepared words that come at the moment.

Expressive prayer is responding to God in a bodily way. It can include singing, dancing, movement, gestures, or creating art.

Contemplative prayer is the response to God's presence that happens within a person when that person is alone with God and experiences God's presence, sometimes beyond words in simple holy silence.

Symbols

Alpha and Omega—The first and last letters of the Greek alphabet which signify that Jesus is the beginning and the end of all things.

Ark and Rainbow—The most common symbol of the flood. Also a symbol of the Church, signifying that the Church is a refuge for all people.

Ark of the Covenant—A small box containing the stone tablets on which the Ten Commandments were inscribed; a symbol of the presence of Yahweh.

Bread and Wine—Symbols of life and of that which nourishes and sustains life. In the Eucharist, these symbols become the sacramental Body and Blood of Christ, His Eucharistic presence.

Burning Bush—Symbol of the call of Moses, who recognized that God was speaking to him from the bush.

Butterfly—Symbol of the resurrection and eternal life.

Chalice—A vessel for the Blood of Christ and so also a symbol of its contents.

Chi Rho—A monogram of the first two letters of the Greek word for Christ.

Circle—A symbol for eternity, because it is without beginning and without end.

Circle and Triangle—A symbol of the eternity of the Trinity.

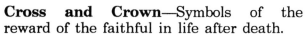

Cross and Crown—Symbols of the reward of the faithful in life after death.

Crown of Thorns—A symbol of the suffering and humiliation suffered by Jesus during his trial before Pilate.

Dove—A symbol of the Holy Spirit and the presence of God.

Dove with Olive Sprig—A symbol of the end of the flood; it denotes peace, forgiveness, and anticipation of new life.

Eagle—A symbol for St. John the Evangelist.

Easter Candle—A symbol of the presence of the Risen Christ.

Eye in the Triangle—The eye symbolizes the all-seeing eye of God; the triangle symbolizes the Trinity.

Fish—A secret sign used by the early Christians to designate themselves as believers in Jesus.

Flames—A symbol often used in the Bible to signify an appearance of God to humanity.

Grapes—Symbolizes the Sacrament of the Eucharist.

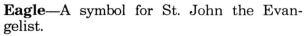
Hand of God, Blesser—Symbol of God the Father as blesser. The three extended fingers suggest the Trinity, and the two closed fingers suggest the twofold nature of Jesus.

Hand of God, Creator—Symbol of the Father as Creator.

Heart and Dagger—Symbol of the sorrows of Mary, Mother of Jesus.

IHS—Symbol for Jesus formed by using the first three letters of the Greek spelling of Jesus.

I.N.R.I.—Initial letters for Latin script on the cross: Jesus of Nazareth, King of the Jews.

Jesse Tree—A symbol designed to recall the greatness of the contribution made under the plan of God, by Jesse, the father of David.

Jesus Monogram—Symbol for Jesus formed by using the first two letters and the last letter of the word *Jesus* in Greek.

Laying on of Hands—A symbol representing the transferring of human or divine power from one person to another; a New Testament and Christian symbol for the sharing of the power of the Holy Spirit.

Lily—Symbol of Easter and immortality.

Menorah—A seven-branch candlestick used in Jewish ritual.

Nimbus—Often called a halo, the nimbus is a symbol of sanctity and is used to denote a person recognized for outstanding holiness.

Oil—A symbol of strength, healing, and mission; for Catholics oil is a symbol of their share in Christ's role as priest, king, and prophet.

Olive Branch—Symbol for peace, harmony, and healing.

Open Bible—Symbol of the Word of God.

PAX—Latin word for peace.

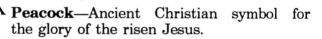 **Peacock**—Ancient Christian symbol for the glory of the risen Jesus.

Sacrificial Lamb—A symbol representing Jesus' offering himself to God to make us one with God.

Scroll—Symbol for the Torah, the first five books of the Old Testament.

Shell with Drops of Water—Symbol of our Lord's baptism.

Shepherd and Lamb—A symbol reminding us of the loving care of Jesus, the Good Shepherd for his people.

Star of David—Traditionally symbolizes the shape of David's shield; symbolic of the Jewish people. Sometimes called the Creator's Star, recalling the six days of creation.

Tablets of Stone—Symbol for the Ten Commandments given to Moses.

Three Intertwining Circles—A symbol of the equality, unity, and co-eternal nature of the Trinity.

Triquetra—Early symbol of the Holy Trinity consisting of a three-cornered figure, especially one with loops interlaced.

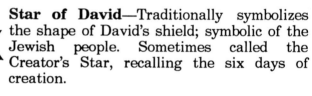 **Water**—A symbol of that which cleanses, sustains, and gives life.

Wheat—Symbolizes Jesus, the Bread of Life.

Winged Lion—Symbol of the evangelist, Mark.

Winged Man—Symbol of the evangelist, Matthew.

Winged Ox—Symbol of the evangelist, Luke.

Crosses

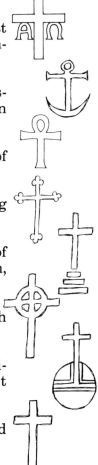

Alpha/Omega Cross—A symbol of Christ as the fullness of redemption, the beginning and the end.

Anchor Cross—Used by the early Christians in the catacombs; ancient Egyptian in origin.

Ankh Cross—The Egyptian symbol of eternal life.

Budded Cross—Symbolizes the young Christian.

Calvary Cross—A cross at the top of three steps symbolizing Jesus' death, rising, and reigning.

Celtic Cross—A cross with a circle, which symbolizes completed redemption.

Cross of Triumph—A symbol of the triumph of Christ and the Gospel throughout the world.

Latin Cross—The most commonly used form of the cross.